SECRET
TORONTO

SECRET TORONTO

The Unique Guidebook
to Toronto's Hidden Sites,
Sounds, & Tastes

Revised Edition

Scott Mitchell

WITH PHOTOGRAPHS BY
Linda Rutenberg

ECW PRESS

The publication of *Secret Toronto* has been generously supported by the Canada Council, the Ontario Arts Council, and the Government of Canada through the Book Publishing Industry Development Program. Canadä

NATIONAL LIBRARY OF CANADA CATALOGUING IN PUBLICATION DATA

Mitchell, Scott, 1959-
Secret Toronto: the unique guidebook to Toronto's hidden sites, sounds & tastes
Rev. ed.
Includes index.
ISBN 1-55022-494-8
I. Toronto (Ont.) — Guidebooks. I. Title.
FC3097.18.M57 2002   917.13'541044   C2001-903590-X
F1059.5T683M58 2002

Original series design: Paul Davies, ECW Type and Art, Oakville, Ontario.
Series editor: Laura Byrne Paquet.
Typesetting: Martel *en-tête.*
Imaging and cover: Guylaine Régimbald – SOLO DESIGN.
Printed by University of Toronto Press.

Distributed in Canada by Stewart House Publishing, Inc.
290 North Queen Street, Suite 210, Etobicoke, Ontario M9C 5K4.

Distributed in the United States by Independent Publishers Group,
814 North Franklin Street, Chicago, Illinois, 60610.

Published by ECW PRESS
2120 Queen Street East, Suite 200, Toronto, Ontario M4E 1E2.

ecwpress.com

PRINTED AND BOUND IN CANADA

TABLE OF CONTENTS

SECRET . . .

INTRODUCTION

This book will lead you astray. Written to reveal lesser known and sometimes entirely obscure facets of Toronto, it will appeal to the adventurous traveler who wants to experience the city's true culture. It invites you to turn a blind eye to famous tourist attractions and to focus instead on the unusual and the undiscovered.

Secret Toronto takes you underground and into unfamiliar neighborhoods. It coaxes you to creep down alleyways, to eat meals unlike anything you've tasted before, to try a new sport, or to sport a new look. Along the way, it offers commentary on Toronto's heritage and advice about tapping into the city's extraordinary artist-run culture. Whether you're visiting Toronto for the first time or you've lived here all your life, you'll find an exciting and unknown city you've never experienced before.

In *Secret Toronto*, I haven't provided prefab tours or planned itineraries. The book should help you set your own agenda, according to your personal quirks and requirements — there's something here for everyone. Unlike most guidebooks, *Secret Toronto* encourages you to wander away from the beaten path. If you find something that piques your curiosity, put the book in your pocket and follow your instincts. You'll come back from your travels with a tale uniquely your own — and a greater appreciation for Toronto and its many hidden pleasures.

The second edition has been thoroughly revised. I've updated addresses and phone numbers for establishments that have moved. A few hidden gems unearthed in the first edition have now gone into permanent hiding, so I've dropped them from the book to make room for new secrets. I've also added new categories — see, for example, "Secret Baseball," "Secret Bonsai," and "Secret Bubble Tea," and that's only the Bs — and included many new restaurant listings for the curious epicure. Ostrich burgers, anyone?

H O W   T O   U S E
SECRET TORONTO

Entries in *Secret Toronto* are arranged alphabetically by subject. This strategy will help you find activities and places that appeal to your own special appetites. Care for a little stargazing? Consult the section on "Secret Astronomy." Looking for a liquid boost? Jump to "Secret Juice Bars." Turned on by shoes, stamps, or sugary sweets? You know where to look. I've included cross-references to alert you to other categories in *Secret Toronto* that may overlap with your interests. The alphabetical and subject indexes at the back of the book will direct you quickly to individual entries.

Every listing includes an address and telephone number. (Note that 10-digit dialing is now the rule everywhere in the Greater Toronto Area, so make sure you use the area code as listed, even for local calls.) Explicit directions, hours of operation, and prices are *not* included, unless there's a good reason. Call ahead if you want to confirm any of those details and, indeed, to make sure that the establishment is still there. Every listing was verified for accuracy at press time, but Toronto is in constant flux, and business, after all, is business — restaurants and shops come and go. On the other hand, if you're feeling adventurous, go ahead and just show up. Maybe you'll make your own secret discovery in a neighborhood you wouldn't otherwise have visited.

OTHER RESOURCES

Toronto's most complete music, film, theater, art, and event listings are published every Thursday in *NOW*, a free paper distributed throughout town at stores, clubs, restaurants, and coffeeshops, as well as in street boxes at major intersections. Be sure to pick up your copy on Thursday or Friday, to avoid missing out on the action, since the listings concentrate on the current week. Other sources for event listings include *eye Weekly*, available free every Thursday, and weekend supplements in the major dailies: the *Globe and Mail*, *National Post*, and the *Toronto Star*, which also publishes a "What's On" guide on Thursday.

Upmarket commentary can be found in the pages of *Toronto Life*, a monthly magazine catering mostly to the opera crowd and urban professionals. Of particular interest to visitors are the restaurant reviews and a regular column revealing the best places to shop, shop, shop. The biweekly *Xtra* covers Toronto's gay and lesbian community. If you've got the family in tow, pick up a copy of *City Parent*, a free monthly tabloid with a calendar of events and a list of kiddy attractions. Look for it in libraries, bookstores, and toy stores. Monthly art gallery listings and a handy street map can be found in *Slate*, available at most galleries and some bookstores. *WholeNote*, a free monthly music magazine, publishes comprehensive listings of classical and contemporary concerts. It's available at most branches of the **Toronto Public Library** (789 Yonge and elsewhere), HMV **Canada** (333 Yonge and elsewhere), and other music shops.

The **Ontario Travel Information Centre** (Eaton Centre, Level 1 Below, 220 Yonge, 416-314-5899), near the Dundas Street entrance to the mall, is open weekdays (10 a.m. to 5 p.m.), Saturday (9:30 a.m. to

6 p.m.), and Sunday (noon to 5 p.m.). Its walls are lined with pamphlets describing attractions, accommodations, and festivals. You can also get flyers and guides from information desks at **Toronto City Hall** (100 Queen West, 416-392-7341) and **Metro Hall** (55 John Street, 416-338-0338). **Tourism Toronto** (416-203-2500, www.torontotourism. com) maintains a live information line during the day if you're looking for mainstream recommendations.

Despite a criminal lack of funding from the provincial government, the **Toronto Transit Commission** (416-393-4636; hearing impaired: 416-481-2523; www.ttc.ca) is still the best way to get around town. Day passes for one person are good for unlimited travel after 9:30 a.m. on weekdays and all day Saturday; Sunday and statutory holiday passes allow one-day unlimited travel for up to six people (maximum two adults). Weekly and monthly passes are also available. Free pocket maps (***Ride Guides***) show subway, bus, streetcar, light rail transit (LRT), and GO routes. Pick one up at a ticket wicket at any subway station, or download an electronic version from the TTC Web site. TTC route and schedule information is also available by phone every day from 7 a.m. to 10 p.m. — in more than 140 languages. For late-night jaunts, don't worry if you miss the last subway train. An after-hours service called the **Blue Night Network** runs buses and streetcars on most major routes from about 1:30 a.m. to 5 a.m., at least every 30 minutes. All-night transit stops are marked with a reflective blue band.

SECRET
ACOUSTICS

In 1987, a little-known Toronto band called Cowboy Junkies married the voice of singer Margo Timmins to the natural acoustics of a little church in downtown Toronto and recorded the groundbreaking *Trinity Sessions* album. Now overshadowed by the mammoth Eaton Centre and easily overlooked, the lovely **Church of the Holy Trinity** (Trinity Square, Yonge and Dundas, accessible from the Eaton Centre exit at the south end of Eaton's or from the park at Bay and Dundas West, 416-598-4521) was once the central fixture of a working-class "suburb" of York known as Macaulay Town. Completed in 1847, Holy Trinity had the distinction of being Toronto's first Anglican church where the pews were entirely free, a condition set by an anonymous benefactor (an Englishwoman whose identity was not revealed until 1898). The rectory and garden of Holy Trinity now offer a secluded, peaceful retreat from the frenetic shopping mall. Services are still celebrated in the church, which hosts plays and concerts, including the annual Christmas pageant (a tradition for more than 60 years).

SECRET
ACTIVISM

Antiracism, Third World politics and development, labor, disarmament, and the women's movement are hot topics at DEC **Bookroom** (836 Bloor West, two blocks east of Ossington, 416-516-2966). This

bright, welcoming store is run by the Development Education Centre, whose mandate includes focusing Canadian attention on global struggles for change. Similarly, the **Centre for Social Justice** (416-516-0009) works to challenge the corporate domination of Canadian politics. Occupying a large space at the back of the DEC Bookroom, the CSJ serves as a meeting place for activists from unions, universities, faith communities, and social movements.

Much smaller and leaning much harder to the left, **Pathfinder Book Store** (2761 Dundas West, 416-767-3705) specializes in titles on socialism and Marxism. It's also a good place to pick up Cuban and Latin American revolutionary newspapers, if you're in that sort of mood. The store is open only for a few hours on Thursday and Friday evenings, and Saturday afternoons, so call ahead to check the schedule or make an appointment.

SECRET
AFRICAN

Upper Canada abolished slavery in 1793, and people of African descent have been settling in Toronto and contributing to the city's economic and cultural growth ever since. North America's first black woman journalist and newspaper editor, Mary Ann Shadd, for example, began her publishing career in Toronto when she founded the *Provincial Freeman* in 1853. The weekly paper promoted the anti-slavery movement and ran stories about black Canadian refugees. And Toronto's first taxi company was owned and operated by an African Canadian. Stories like these form the fabric of historical tours of Toronto organized by the **Ontario Black History Society** (10 Adelaide East, Suite 202, 416-867-9420, www.blackhistorysociety. ca). A three-hour tour explores 15 different sites and includes opportunities to shop at black-owned businesses. Shorter excursions can also be arranged. All tours begin and end at the office on Adelaide, where the society maintains a small but significant reference library.

The **Ashanti Room** (28 Lennox, near Bloor and Bathurst, 416-588-3934) is filled with djmbe drums from Ghana, hand-carved Ashanti stools, and beautiful dyed and designed fabrics from Zimbabwe, South Africa, Mali, and other African nations. This shop — formerly a house, with the wooden panels and molding still intact — also devotes an entire room to cards, coloring books, black literature, and Afrocentric educational material, while the upper floor offers jewelry, more furnishings, and a room set aside for reflexology treatments.

The **Charles Mus Gallery** (156 Davenport, at Bay, 416-921-5870) is both gallery and bookstore, offering thematic exhibitions that focus on individual cultures or the work of contemporary African artists, as well as displays of masks, shields, textiles, and other traditional artifacts. If something's not physically present, you're sure to find a printed representation in one of the many books in stock. The store specializes in ethnographic titles spanning a wide range of cultures, from African, Amerindian, and Inuit to Islamic and Southeast Asian.

It rains almost every year at **Afrofest in the Park** (Queen's Park, Wellesley West and Queen's Park Crescent), but that never dampens the spirit of this free day-long festival in early July. The bands keep playing sunny rhythms, and the crowd just kicks off their shoes and dances in the wet grass, while vendors selling African jewelry, T-shirts, and homemade meals set up stalls under the huge trees. Meanwhile, a Sunday-afternoon concert in the park is the grand finale of a week of entertainment organized by **Music Africa** (416-

469-5336), which brings some of the best African performers to town.

At **B's Place African Cuisine** (2133 Jane, south of Wilson, 416-242-8858), Esther Adeolu prepares dishes typical of Nigeria and Ghana, including fufu (mashed yam and plantain dumplings), fish and spinach stew, deep-fried plantains, and bean soup. Tucked into a strip mall on busy Jane Street, the restaurant isn't big on atmosphere, but if you don't mind the big-screen TV and the bright lights, you'll enjoy the authentic tastes.

French, African, and Creole flavors meet in the cuisine of Mauritius, a small island in the Indian Ocean. The resulting hot masala is reflected in the menu at **Blue Bay Café** (2243 Dundas West, south of Bloor, 416-533-8838), where choices include snapper in a sauce of garlic, onion, and yellow mustard seed, spicy chicken stew, and sautéed beef with tomato and okra.

SECRET
AFTER HOURS

Cowboy boots are no longer de rigueur at the **Matador Club** (466 Dovercourt, at College, 416-533-9311), Toronto's oldest after-hours dance venue, despite the clutch of finely embroidered nosepickers decorating the stage — not to mention the moose antlers, signed mug shots, and other country music memorabilia collected over the years by club owner Ann Dunn. Nashville notables like Johnny Cash, Conway Twitty, Ian Tyson, and Loretta Lynn used to hang out at the Mat, back when the music was strictly country of the fiddle-and-steel-guitar variety. Nowadays, the live bands on Friday and Saturday nights — when the club opens from 1:30 a.m. to 5:30 a.m. — tend to play a blend of standard rock covers (Kinks, Doors, Creedence Clearwater Revival) and current faves (such as Canada's own Alanis Morissette or The Tragically Hip). But the after-hours crowd still shows up for the same reason they've been coming here since 1964: to kick up their heels on the big hardwood dance floor. Constructed as a dance hall for restless soldiers during the First World War, the building was later reincarnated as a bowling alley before being restored to its original purpose. In 1992, Canadian balladeer-cum-Zen-poet Leonard Cohen penned the tune "Closing Time" in honor of the club and filmed the video version inside its cavernous confines. The place is unlicensed, but the coffeeshop just inside the door serves soft drinks and bottled water, as well as burritos and fresh chili to give you strength for more floor pounding. Closing time comes quickly, but before you leave, pick up some souvenir kitsch at the little gift stand, or pose for a Polaroid snap. The Matador is all about memories — making new ones or reveling in old ones.

S E C R E T
ANTIQUES
⊰⊱

Toronto has hundreds of antique stores — although some people might argue that many of these places should properly be labeled junk shops. Nevertheless, there are genuine antique treasures to be found among the merely old and dusty stuff (not to mention some very nice secondhand furniture). Happily, there are several areas in town where antique vendors have clustered in significant numbers to form small communities.

The well-publicized **Harbourfront Antique Market** (390 Queen's Quay West, just south of SkyDome, 416-260-2626), with more than 100 independent dealers wedged into one edifice, caters largely to the tourist trade — and the price tags often reflect that fact. Open Tuesday to Sunday, and some holiday Mondays, the market also hosts silent auctions and special events. The best time to go is a summer Sunday, however, when the selling spills over to an outdoor market, set up under canopies on the south side of Queen's Quay just east of the permanent market. Both local and out-of-town vendors unpack their vans in the lakeside lot, attracting families and other fun-seekers from nearby Harbourfront Centre. Don't be afraid to haggle for something you really like — many dealers would rather lower the price than reload the van.

Parkdale has been home for years to a loose-knit community of antique dealers, hunkered down in a hodgepodge strip of greasy spoons and rundown little bric-a-brac shops along Queen Street West between Triller and Roncesvalles. **Sam the Chandelier Man** (1633 Queen West, 416-537-9707) is one of the permanent fixtures (if you'll pardon the pun), with a rambling collection of lampshades and hard-to-find parts. The lamp assemblage has grown to occupy not only two stores but also additional window display space just up the street. Nearby, a number of other dealers share space in a large building, possibly a movie theater when first built but now known as the **Queen West Antique Centre** (1605 Queen West, at Triller, 416-588-2212). Almost every store on the opposite side of the street is now an antique shop of some sort, and most of the owners in this neighborhood have banded together to market themselves as the **Sunnyside Antique Community**. The name derives from the now-defunct boardwalk amusement park that once lay directly south of the Queen-Roncesvalles junction, and it harks back to a happier, now historic era (see "Secret Sunnyside").

In the other direction, along Queen Street East between Pape and Jones, you'll find another little vintage and antique district, in the area known as Leslieville. This is not a particularly affluent area of town, and the antiques are outnumbered by pure junk and fab '50s kitsch, but the neighborhood is struggling to its feet. **Ethel** (1091 Queen East, 416-778-6608) revels in the ephemera of "20th-century living." This is the place to go if you're looking for a cocktail shaker to match the one you remember from your uncle's rec-room bar or perhaps an elegant teak coffee table with a simple, midcentury Scandinavian design. Ethel owners Greg Perras and Craig Soper, who live above the shop, are leading the Danish modern revival. More furniture and collectibles can be found at **EyeSpy** (1100 Queen West, 416-461-4061), where owner Teré Ouellette has an especially fond eye for ceramics, including Russel Wright dishes and cookie jars by McCoy (a favorite item of Andy Warhol's). Flea-market furniture shoppers will enjoy poking around in both basements and the over-crowded main-floor rooms at **All Most Antiques** (1150 Queen East, 416-466-9724). The stash is almost all junk, but the store stays open seven days a week. Respite and refreshment lie just east of Jones, at **Tango Palace Coffee Co.** (1156 Queen East, 416-465-8085), where the atmosphere is relaxed, and the sweets counter is fully stocked.

Of course, Queen Street antique stores aren't confined to these two neighborhoods in the east and west. There are many shops in between (and beyond, as far east as the Beaches). If you're trundling from one end to the other, a good place to take a break is the trendy Queen West neighborhood, where you'll find an abundance of cafés and restaurants. Among the many retro junk shops in the stretch west of

Bathurst, **Mostly Movables** (785 Queen West, 416-504-4455) stands out for its wardrobes, dressers, and dining room sets, often refinished or reupholstered in the back room and selling for reasonable prices.

Upscale shoppers will find more shops uptown, conveniently clustered along Mount Pleasant Road for several blocks immediately south of Eglinton. Victorian furniture, oodles of china, silver, and glass, and "objets d'art" are the province of overstuffed **Bernardi's Antiques** (699 Mount Pleasant, 416-483-6471), while **Sharon O'Dowd Antiques** (606 Mount Pleasant, 416-322-0927) specializes in "country furnishings." Resembling a well-organized attic — or, rather, a well-furnished barn loft — the 8,000-square-foot **Horsefeathers** (630 Mount Pleasant, 416-486-4555) specializes in furniture and rare fancies from England and France. Despite the address, the entrance is actually around the corner, off the small parking lot on Manor Road — so don't misguidedly wander into the linen shop out front on Mount Pleasant (unless you're looking for new linens, of course). Just east of Mount Pleasant, **The Bead Goes On** (256 Soudan, 416-481-7622) buys and sells costume jewelry. Less cleverly named, but certainly more cluttered and constantly ticking, **The Store Antiques** (588 Mount Pleasant, 416-483-2366) sells clocks and small furniture.

SECRET
ARCHITECTURE

Toronto has a terrible habit of knocking down beautiful buildings to make way for new developments. Years ago, when various city structures suffered the weight of the wrecking ball, remnants were rescued and preserved in Spencer Clark's unusual collection of sculpture and architectural fragments, now strategically scattered about the grounds and gardens of the **Guild Inn** (191 Guildwood Parkway, Scarborough, 416-261-3331). Perched on the crest of the Scarborough Bluffs (see "Secret Scarborough"), the inn was originally the Guild of All Arts, an artists' colony founded in 1932 by Clark and his wife, Rosa. Clark's menagerie of more than 300 ornaments and artifacts includes a stone-and-wrought-iron Bank of Nova Scotia entranceway, Ionic columns and arches from several other banks, sculptured panels from the *Globe and Mail* building, an old log cabin, a belfry, and other oddities. Guided tours can be arranged. The Guild Inn is located on 90 acres of woodland, approximately 25 minutes east of downtown Toronto.

While you're free to admire the exterior architecture of any building in town, you won't often have the chance to see past the public façade. For those who believe that structural beauty is more than skin deep, **Doors Open Toronto** (www.doorsopen.org) offers a weekend's worth of intimate encounters with roughly 100 historic or architecturally significant buildings. Organized by the City of Toronto Culture Division, in cooperation with local heritage organizations, the annual event occurs on the last weekend in May. While some locations are open to the public year round, many others are normally off limits. Admission is free, and each building presents its own program for visitors, including behind-the-scenes tours, photo exhibits, concerts, lectures, and demonstrations. The *Toronto Star* publishes a complete schedule a week before the event, or you can check the Web site for advance information.

The **Toronto Region Architectural Conservancy** (10 Adelaide East, 416-947-1066) organizes guided tours of city landmarks still standing — and works to keep them that way. Call to find out about upcoming events, or put your name on the mailing list for advance notification.

Ballenford Books on Architecture (600 Markham, just south of Bloor, at Bathurst, 416-588-0800) specializes in architecture and urban design titles, on subjects as diverse as Bavarian rococo, gardens of the French Riviera, and landmarks of Soviet architecture. One wall of the store is dedicated to displays of architectural drawings.

SECRET
ARCHIVES

Determined to do away with the mistaken idea that archival collections are housed in dusty attics and damp basements, the **Metro Toronto Archives and Records Centre** (255 Spadina Road, one block north of the Dupont subway, 416-392-5564) welcomes visitors into its state-of-the-art facility. Large viewing windows allow visual access to the astounding climate-controlled stacks — boxes and boxes of Metro records you can request for closer examination in the second-floor Research Hall. Several permanent exhibits, including *Archives in the Information Age* and the 22-minute multi-image slide program *Metro Perspectives*, introduce archival concepts and highlight the importance of urban history. Excellent changing exhibits focus on historical themes specific to Metro, including heritage preservation, expressways, sewer pipes, and the effects of planning decisions in the past century on the development of neighborhoods and urban sprawl. Located within view of Casa Loma, on land originally marked for the controversial Spadina Expressway (canceled in 1971), the Metro Archives takes a decidedly lively approach to history. Arrange free tours for groups of 10 or more by calling 416-397-7977. Incidentally, the small theater is also the site of several community events, including the Toronto Symphony's annual spring piano competition.

From seeds planted in 1973, when a few Torontonians started preserving physical evidence of gay culture in this country, the **Canadian Lesbian and Gay Archives** (56 Temperance, Suite 201, west of Bay, 416-777-2755) have grown into an astonishingly rich resource. Run entirely by volunteers, the CLGA began as a filing cabinet full of clippings at the now-defunct *Body Politic* (Canada's gay newsmagazine of record) and currently comprises not only the world's largest collection of gay and lesbian periodicals and several thousand books but also posters, photos, protest buttons, films, artworks, and audio and video recordings. Open Tuesday, Wednesday, and Thursday evenings between 7:30 p.m. and 10 p.m. or by appointment. The front door of the building is usually locked, so press the archives button, and someone will buzz you in.

Located upstairs from the South St. Lawrence Market, the **Market Gallery of the City of Toronto Archives** (95 Front East, at Jarvis, second floor, 416-392-7604) mounts changing displays that vividly recall aspects of the city's history and culture. The photographs, maps, paintings, documents, and physical artifacts are drawn from Toronto's official fine art and archival collections. Located within easy walking distance of both King and Union subway stations, the Market Gallery shares the neighborhood with many historic landmarks, such as the Cathedral Church of St. James (see "Secret Gothic") and the unique Gooderham Building (see "Secret Elevators").

Film buffs will appreciate the excellent collection of movie stills, books about film, and press clippings housed at the **Cinematheque**

Ontario Film Reference Library (2 Carlton, 416-967-1517). If you don't mind the price, the library also offers a reproduction service for stills.

S E C R E T

ART BOOKS

You can buy hard-to-find artists' books and videos, plastic pop-culture artifacts, and critical writing like Jeanne Randolph's *Symbolization and Its Discontents*, as well as media-related and multiple-format work, at **Art Metropole** (788 King West, second floor, 416-703-4400), which doubles as a bookstore and exhibition space.

High on the west wall of **David Mirvish Books** (595 Markham, south of Bloor, 416-531-9975), a permanently installed painting by Frank Stella presides over the buyers below. Left over from the bookstore's former incarnation as an avant-garde art gallery, and perhaps just too big to go anywhere else, *Damascus Gate Stretch Variation I* (1970) does indeed stretch — it's a full 50 feet across. Most of the store's floor space is occupied by low tables where hundreds of discount books are displayed faceup for easy browsing. Weekly sales are advertised in the local papers, and Sunday early birds can pick up a copy of the *Sunday New York Times* at slightly less than the going rate.

The **Art Gallery of Ontario Book Shop** (317 Dundas West, 416-979-6610), directly behind the ground-level café, occupies only a fraction of the gallery's large space devoted to merchandising. But the selection of art books — on topics from anatomy and art criticism to museology and printmaking — befits a major gallery. In keeping with the AGO's emphasis on education (art classes and school tours are an integral part of the gallery's program), the bookshop has a children's section, including pedagogical CD-ROMs.

Devoted to out-of-print and secondhand art books, **Acadia Art and Rare Books** (232 Queen East, near Sherbourne, 416-364-7638) is a great place to find monographs, exhibition catalogs, and limited-edition titles, often containing original lithographs. Upstairs, where the rare and leather-bound books are kept, the owner has amassed a fantastic collection of antique prints, including maps and botanical drawings.

S E C R E T

ART DECO

You might think you've wandered onto an abandoned movie set from some 1930s Hollywood epic when you first encounter the **R.C. Harris Filtration Plant** (2701 Queen East, at Victoria Park, 416-392-3566), but this opulent Art Deco palace overlooking Lake Ontario is a functioning waterworks, supplying 45 percent of the water to residents in Metro and York Region. The plant represents a rare fusion of innovative engineering and architectural elegance. Marble floors and bronze fittings suggest the interior of a temple, and indeed this reverential treatment inspired Toronto novelist Michael Ondaatje to weave the historical account of the plant's construction into his fictional tale *In the Skin of Lion*. He concludes with a description of the "unfloored high windows" overlooking "filter pools four feet deep, languid, reflective as medieval water gardens." You can step inside this

dream for a one-hour guided tour on Saturday (10 a.m., 11:30 a.m., and 1 p.m.) or other days by appointment. The Saturday walk-in tours are very popular and tend to fill up fast. You can't reserve a spot, so just show up early. Enter the grounds through the gate on Queen Street and follow the curving road right to the bottom of the hill (look for the tour sign by the door nearest the parking lot). The open green space along the lakeshore is also a nice spot for picnicking, and it's a favorite dog walk for residents of the surrounding neighborhoods, including the Beaches immediately west of the plant.

Downtown at the southwest corner of Yonge and College, the distinctive seven-story **College Park** building (444 Yonge, 416-597-1221) was something of an architectural event when it was constructed in 1928–30. The T. Eaton Company, having outgrown the warren of workrooms, offices, and retail space at its original location farther south on Yonge Street, envisioned a soaring 40-story Art Deco skyscraper at the new College location, but the Depression intervened. Still, the part they managed to build is impressive. When the famous retailer relocated again in 1977, moving into the new, deliberately brutal Eaton Centre at Yonge and Dundas (architecturally designed to expose the elevator shafts, ductwork, and structural elements, including steel beams and poured concrete), the College Street building was carved up into smaller shops. Fortunately, much of the original interior elegance of College Park is still visible. The seventh-floor restaurant and delicious Art Deco concert hall — once home to the Women's Musical Club of Toronto, but closed to the public and gathering dust for 25 years — will soon be restored and reopened.

Aficionados of Art Deco artifacts will want to browse the furniture and accessories at **Red Indian Art Deco** (536 Queen West, 416-504-7706) and the amazing collection at Jake Keck's **Machine Age Modern** (1000 Queen East, 416-461-3588).

SECRET
ASTRONOMY

The **Petrie Observatory** (Petrie Science Building, York University, 4700 Keele, at Steeles, 416-736-5249, recorded message 416-736-2100, ext. 77773) offers Wednesday-evening stargazing sessions. Put your eye to the 30-cm and 60-cm (one-foot and two-foot) telescopes, and ogle the moon or some other night-sky phenomenon, according to the season. There's a simultaneous slide show, and graduate or undergraduate astronomy students are on hand to entertain questions. The weekly sessions are free, but call ahead to make sure the observatory's open and to check viewing times. The observatory is not wheelchair accessible (there are stairs to climb), and it's open to the elements, so wear your mittens in winter. To get there, take the York University 106 bus from the Downsview subway. If you drive, public parking is available in lot 5A; the Petrie Science Building is due south and visible from the parking lot.

In operation as part of the University of Toronto for more than 60 years, the **David Dunlap Observatory** (123 Hillsview, Richmond Hill, 905-884-2112) houses the largest optical telescope in Canada (185 cm). On Saturday evenings from April through September, the observatory offers a lecture and slide presentation, followed by a visit to the dome. Tickets are only a few dollars, but you must make reservations (a suggested three weeks in advance). No children under seven are permitted. Built in memory of her late husband by Jessie Dunlap, the observatory sits amidst 100 acres of unspoiled natural surroundings, on a site chosen by the benefactor. The town of Richmond Hill has since grown up around it, but a unique light-pollution bylaw keeps the local candlepower in check so that nighttime observing is unaffected. Take the Bayview GO bus from the Finch subway, and ask the driver to stop at Hillsview Drive, just north of 16th Avenue. The observatory is a 10- or 15-minute walk west of Bayview Avenue, but you should call ahead for detailed directions — and be aware that it's quite a trek from downtown Toronto.

The Starlab program in the small planetarium at the **Ontario Science Centre** (770 Don Mills, 416-696-3127) focuses on the current night sky. Moon rocks and meteorites are displayed in the Hall of Space, where visitors can sit in a rocket chair that rides on a cushion of air or put on flight vests and join a simulated space mission. The Science Centre is particularly appealing to kids, and every student within a hundred-mile radius of Toronto is delivered here on a class trip at least once during a school career. (The favorite "scientific" activity I recall from my youth was spontaneous generation of static electricity, accomplished by removing my shoes and dragging sock-footed down the long carpeted corridors, then finding a classmate to shock.) Hundreds of exhibits relating to all aspects of science will keep you busy all day pushing buttons and pulling levers, interacting with computers, and watching multimedia presentations. The nifty gift shop may take almost as much time to enjoy.

Observation workshops, star parties, and lectures on such topics as "Forgotten Globular Clusters" are among the many activities of the **Royal Astronomical Society of Canada, Toronto Centre** (100 Queen's Park, 416-724-7827). Most meetings take place at the Ontario Science Centre (770 Don Mills, 416-696-3127).

If group gazing appeals to you, then don't miss **Starfest**, Canada's largest annual observation convention and star party. Organized by the **North York Astronomical Association** (www.nyaa-starfest. com), the activities include observation sessions, slide presentations, workshops, commercial exhibits, and a children's program. The mid-

August get-together in Mount Forest attracts hundreds of astronomy enthusiasts from all over North America. Members of the NYAA, a small and informal group of folks who share an interest in watching the night sky, meet for other activities throughout the year, such as group observation sessions, workshops, and dark-sky camping weekends.

While funding cuts finally forced the McLaughlin Planetarium to close after 27 years of entertaining and educational star shows — remember the planetarium scene in *Rebel without a Cause*? — the **Royal Ontario Museum** (100 Queen's Park, 416-586-5549) next door continues to offer occasional astronomy programs through its education department (416-586-5797 for course and lecture tickets). Need to know which planetary bodies are ascending? Call 416-586-8000 and follow the touch-tone menu for a recorded message describing the configuration of planets and stars in the current night sky.

EfstonScience (3350 Dufferin, 416-787-4581) and the **Not in My Backyard Astronomers** club host outdoor viewing sessions at the Albion Hills Conservation Area (on Highway 50, north of Bolton). These popular evening events, which regularly attract between 50 and 100 enthusiasts, are held every month from March to November, during two five-day "windows" leading up to the first quarter moon and during the last quarter moon. Don't worry if you don't own a telescope or binoculars, because many of the regulars will happily invite you to take a peek through their own equipment. Call for dates, details, and directions to the conservation area, or drop by the store, located across from Yorkdale Shopping Centre (Yorkdale subway) — just look for the giant telescope on the roof. EfstonScience, whose motto is "Serving Observing," is the largest scientific and astronomy retailer in Canada, and a visit to the shop is a fun excursion on its own.

Inspired by the return of Halley's comet in 1986, amateur astronomer Ray Khan founded **Khan Scope Centre** (3243 Dufferin, three blocks south of Yorkdale, 416-783-4140). The store carries a bevy of high-quality telescopes, as well as binoculars new and used, microscopes, books, and software. Staff members offer classes on how to locate and identify major constellations and planets.

SECRET

AUCTIONS

Every Tuesday at 11 a.m., furniture, collectibles, and other affordable old stuff goes on the block at **Ritchie's Auctioneers and Appraisers** (288 King East, 416-364-1864). Drop in on Monday from 2 p.m. to 7 p.m. for a preview of the next day's treasures. Ritchie's also holds quarterly auctions devoted to jewelry and watches, silver, carpets, ceramics, dolls, and so on, as well as twice-yearly art auctions and occasional specialized sales.

Junk collectors and treasure hunters gather on Saturday afternoons to bid for items in two separate events at the main **Goodwill** thrift store (234 Adelaide East, 416-366-2083). The "as is" department, located in the basement of the side building behind the parking lot, puts an eclectic selection of broken-down odds and sods on the block at 1 p.m. On the second floor of the main building, the furniture bidding begins at 2 p.m. Preview the goods all week during regular hours.

Twice a year, in the spring and fall, used computers and office equipment, cars, and other surplus materials from the municipal government are sold at auction. For dates and details, call the **City of Toronto Auction Information Line** (416-392-1991). Police department auctions are a great place to pick up a cheap two-wheeler recovered by the cops, since Toronto is the number one city in North America for bike theft. Find out more by calling the **Public Auction Info Line** (416-808-3749).

S E C R E T

BACKYARD PATIOS

Dine on the upper back deck at **Kensington Kitchen** (124 Harbord, west of Spadina, 416-961-3404), and you'll feel like you're eating in a tree house. It is lovely and secluded in summer, a perfect place to enjoy some of Toronto's best Middle Eastern food: baba ganouj, tabbouleh salad, dolmades, meshwi, lamb burgers, and brochettes.

Not many restaurants on the Queen West strip have space for backyard tables, so it's not surprising that the courtyard is quaintly small at the **Queen Mother Café** (206 Queen West, at McCaul, 416-598-4719). Getting there, however, requires an underground detour — take the narrow stairs down to the washrooms and follow the basement passage all the way back, and then up again, to emerge behind the kitchen into a pleasant enclosure. The menu at the Queen Mum favors Laotian salads, Thai chicken and shrimp stir-fry dishes, and plenty of coriander and coconut milk, but there's also a decent veggie burger and a tempting dessert bar.

S E C R E T
BAKERIES

The best challah in town comes from **Harbord Bakery** (115 Harbord, west of Spadina, 416-922-5767). In fact, all the breads baked here are worth writing home about. The cooler is stocked with bottled soups, Mendel's cream cheese, and hand-wrapped packages of heavenly smoked salmon, while the sweeter side of the shop displays decadent Florentines, ethereal mandlebrot (almond cookies that resemble biscotti, without the extreme density), and fantastic apple cake.

From its humble beginnings in a small bake house in Caledon, Ontario, in 1982, **Ace Bakery** (1 Hafis, near Keele and Lawrence, 416-241-3600) has grown to serve more than 350 restaurants, hotels, and retail outlets, as well as airlines and caterers. Seventeen different breads, from baguettes to olive boules, are handmade from all-natural ingredients. You won't find them any fresher than here at the main bakery and retail outlet, where they also serve homemade soups, sandwiches, and cookies.

Resistance is futile once you've laid eyes on the array of pecan pies, white chocolate cookies, and other fresh desserts piled high along the counter of **My Market Bakery** (172 Baldwin, west of Spadina, 416-593-6772). And even if you manage to sidle into the shop with your back to the baked goods, you'll find yourself facing the bread rack, where the sourdough olive, potato and leek, and Japanese spice bread with wasabi will convince you that it may indeed be possible to live on bread alone. My Market Bakery epitomizes Kensington Market's appeal to the senses.

A little bit of the Old World lingers on at **Granowska's Bakery** (175 Roncesvalles, 416-533-7755), a well-windowed corner spot stocked with rows of bread, puff pastries, and baked goods filled with plum preserve. The bakery bustles on market day, and you may have trouble getting a table if you want to stay for a coffee, but there's more room when the outdoor café opens during warm-weather months.

S E C R E T

BARBECUED CHICKEN

Don't be surprised if there's a lineup for chicken at the take-out counter of **Churrasqueira Costa Verde** (370 Oakwood, at Rogers, 416-658-9577), where the Portuguese rotisserie-style birds are always perfectly tender. Costa Verde also does half chickens on an open grill — slightly drier, but still delicious, and the waiting list is usually shorter.

Bairrada Churrasqueira (1000 College, west of Dovercourt, 416-539-8239) does their chicken a little differently: split open on vertical racks in a roasting oven, then snipped into pieces with large shears, basted with sweet or hot sauce, and served with generous portions of potato and string beans and a handful of black and green olives. Suckling pig is also a specialty — look for the inside wall mural, a pretty good likeness of the owner (albeit in younger days) handling a spit at the oven door. On the seafood side of the menu, Bairrada cooks codfish half a dozen ways. This is a favorite spot with Portuguese families, and the licensed backyard patio is always busy in summer.

Another popular fowl emporium, where the basting sauces are homemade, is **Churrasco of St. Clair**, now in two locations (679 St. Clair West, near Christie, 416-658-0652; 1104 Bloor West, at Dufferin, 416-533-3199). Accompany your meal with rice and peas or excellent little round roasted potatoes. Take-out service only.

S E C R E T
BARS

The prime reason to visit **Allen's** (143 Danforth, east of Broadview, 416-463-3086) is the fine selection of single malts and the long, long list of beers, both bottled and draft. Wooden booths at the front, a secluded, willow-draped summer patio at the back, and plenty of tables with blue-checked cloths in between — choose a spot to sit, sip your Guinness or Glengoyne, and relax. The atmosphere is reassuringly old-fashioned, with a menu to match (the liver's a good choice). Allen's also serves a decent brunch, distinguished by peameal bacon, tea biscuits, and jam. There's a jukebox well stocked with R&B, while live Celtic and East Coast music every Tuesday and Saturday evening draws a crowd that sometimes threatens to break the floor joists with stomping.

Just around the western bend of College Street before Grace, on the quiet fringe of hipness, **Souz Dal** (636 College, 416-537-1883) offers an intimately darkened environment for consuming late-night margaritas and tapas. The restaurant's name is cut with a welding torch from a rusted metal globe that hangs over the sidewalk, while the teensy patio out back is more like a shed without a roof. It all adds up.

S E C R E T

BASEBALL

Annual attendance at Blue Jays games in Toronto has dwindled by a million fans (make that ex-fans) in the past decade, so unless the Blue Jays come seriously close to winning the World Series pennant again (as they did with back-to-back victories in 1992 and 1993), you'll never have any trouble buying a decent seat for a game at SkyDome. But why pay at all — and why pay extortionate prices for a hot dog — when you can enjoy a free game, and cheap dogs, at **Christie Pits** (Bloor West and Christie)? This 20-acre park, formerly a sand and gravel pit — and the site of Toronto's first race riot, in 1933, when a swastika flag was unfurled at a softball game between Jewish and non-Jewish teams — now has three diamonds, a skating rink, an outdoor swimming pool, soccer fields, and plenty of play space. The **Toronto Maple Leafs Baseball Club** (416-631-2600, www. mapleleafsbaseball.com) — and no, I'm not confusing it with the somewhat better known hockey team — plays a regular season here every summer, from May through July. The Leafs are frequent winners in the Inter-County Major Baseball League. Established in 1919, the league now includes teams from Barrie, Brantford, Guelph, Hamilton, Kitchener, London, Stratford, St. Thomas, and Waterloo. Home-game spectators at Christie Pits can get close enough to push their noses through the batting cage, if they want. Most people choose to take a higher view, parking their lawn chairs at the top of the steep embankment overlooking the park. It still beats the nose-bleed seats at SkyDome, even if there isn't a Jumbotron for instant replays. Team owners Jack and Lynn Dominico are often at the game, selling cheap raffle tickets for inexpensive prizes (boxes of gum or packs of baseball cards) to raise money for the league. Baseball history buffs will know that there's been a Toronto Maple Leafs Baseball Club for more than a century, playing from 1897 at Hanlan's Point Amusement Park on the Toronto Islands and later at Maple Leaf Park at the foot of Bathurst Street. It was there, on September 5, 1914, that 19-year-old George Herman "Babe" Ruth, playing for the Providence Grays against the Maple Leafs, scored his first professional home run, knocking the ball clear out of the park into the bay.

S E C R E T

BEACH VOLLEYBALL

There's no need to go south in winter anymore for a romp in the sand. **Beach Blast** (15 Leswyn, near Lawrence West and Caledonia, 416-785-6677) has six full-size indoor volleyball courts, carpeted with more than 1,200 tons of sand and warmed by radiant-heat tubes that do a good job of mimicking the sun. Occupying a converted steel-bridge factory, this climate-controlled playground comes complete with a cedar boardwalk and licensed bar. You can book a court for $90 an hour, and you don't need to wear sunscreen. Don't confuse this leisure-time activity with grueling Olympic-style beach volleyball, where the court must be covered by a two-person team. At Beach Blast, you're encouraged to book the court for groups of 20, so you can rotate out and stroll to the bar. The courts are open all year, but weekday evenings are usually booked for league play, so call ahead to find out what's available. Beach Blast has also opened a second location, with seven courts, at **The Docks** entertainment complex by the lake (11 Poulson, 416-222-3577).

SECRET
BEDTIME STORIES

If you've reread the stories of Winnie the Pooh and Paddington Bear more times than you can remember, you may be looking for some new material. Luckily, Toronto caters well to young book lovers. **Mabel's Fables, the Story Book Store** (662 Mount Pleasant, near Eglinton, 416-322-0438) creates a kid-friendly environment with stuffed animals and seating for young readers. Attentive employees provide knowledgeable recommendations for any age or reading level.

The white lace curtains and brass lamps at **The Constant Reader** (111 Harbord, west of Spadina, 416-972-0661) fit well with the store's reverent attitude toward reading and small collection of antiquarian books for children. New and used titles include anthologies, fairy tales, and folklore, with an emphasis on the arts and multicultural literature.

Just a hop, skip, and jump to the west, **Parentbooks** (201 Harbord, at Bathurst, 416-537-8334) has a small selection of storybooks. Most of the shelf space, however, is devoted to books for parents and professional caregivers, counselors, therapists, educators, and clinicians. The tiny store stocks more than 15,000 titles on topics ranging from childbirth and infant care to education, health, parenting skills, and psychology.

SECRET

BEER

Several English-style ales, including Peculiar (a dark ale styled after a North Yorkshire brew sometimes known as "lunatic broth") and the seasonal Keefe's Irish Stout, are brewed at the **Granite Brewery** (245 Eglinton East, at Mount Pleasant, 416-322-0723). If you're eating, ask the staff to recommend a beer to match or contrast with your meal. There are front and back patios for drinking al fresco, and brewery tours are available when the brewer is in. (When he's not, you can still take a peek at the copper kettles through glass display windows.) Watch for periodic special events such as the Brewers' Banquet, featuring all-inclusive meals cooked or coupled with various beers. Granite has a second spot, the smaller and cozier **Beer Street** (729 Danforth, at Pape, 416-405-8100), where you can get the same great ales (brewed at the original location).

The **Amsterdam Brewing Company** (600 King West, at Portland, 416-504-6882 [brewery], 416-504-1040 [retail store]) supplies its popular Natural Blonde and Nut Brown Ale to bars and beer stores, but its other (and frankly better) brews are only available onsite. You can buy bottles of Dutch Amber and Framboise, as well as various seasonals, at the retail store, or enjoy them on tap at the long bar under the brewery. Pop by on Sunday at 2 p.m. (or by appointment) for an official tour of the glassed-in brewery, followed by free samples. The Amsterdam used to run a bigger brew pub on John Street, one of the first in Toronto, but closed it to focus on the brewing operation. The pub reopened under new owners as **Al Frisco's** (133 John Street, 416-595-8201), with the original equipment in place. They brew a couple of their own beers but nothing to match Amsterdam's.

Beer nuts wandering east of Yonge Street will appreciate **Denison's Brewing Company** (75 Victoria, 416-360-5877), where they brew only high-quality, Bavarian-style lagers. The brew masters are strict adherents to the "Reinheitsgebot," a German law governing beer purity enacted in 1516 by Wilhelm IV. Housed in historic digs, Denison's is actually a cluster of three establishments built around a multilevel glassed-in brewery: Crazy Louie's Brasserie and Conchy Joe's upstairs, and Growler's Pub in the basement. Drop by after work or a night at the theater, and take a self-guided tour of the brewing process.

Laid-back **C'est What?** (67 Front West or 19 Church, 416-867-9499) offers an impressive selection of microbrews on tap and ferments a few of its own onsite. Their most famous brand is Coffee Porter, described by some as "dark and chewy," with a distinct taste of coffee bean. C'est What? brings in live bands almost every night (enter from Church Street for the live music). On the quieter pub side of the establishment, there's a stack of board games, from backgammon to Battleship, to keep you amused.

Debuting in March 2000, the German-style Steam Whistle Pilsner was the first beer to emerge from **Steam Whistle Brewing** (The Roundhouse, 255 Bremner, 416-362-2337). Steam Whistle is a new company launched by Cameron Heaps, son of Upper Canada Brewing Company founder Frank Heaps. (Upper Canada left Toronto a few years back when Sleeman bought it.) The microbrewery is located south of SkyDome in the historic **John Street Roundhouse**, a horseshoe-shaped building erected by the Canadian Pacific Railway in 1929 as a storage and maintenance facility. There's still a working steam whistle onsite. The brewery, including a retail store, occupies about a third of the building. Tentative city plans would see a railway museum built in the remaining space, and several vintage rail cars and locomotives are already stored inside. In the meantime, railway buffs can enjoy a stroll around the exterior. Back inside, Steam Whistle offers public tours that include a history of the Roundhouse, a walk through the brewery, and follow-up sips at the tasting bar. The 20-minute tours run every hour, seven days a week, and cost only $2 per person (souvenir glass included).

Toronto's Festival of Beer (1-877-427-0235) is a weekend-long affair in early August that brings together more than 30 microbreweries. Held outdoors at historic Fort York (see "Secret History"), the festival features workshops, speakers, live jazz and blues, and plenty of beverages. Children, dogs, and nondrinkers are welcome.

The brewery at **Todmorden Mills Heritage Museum and Arts Centre** (67 Pottery, just west of Broadview at Mortimer, 416-396-2819) reminds us that beer-making was a popular enterprise for Toronto pioneers. Located in the Don Valley, Todmorden also has a paper mill (formerly a grist mill), several restored houses from the late 18th and early 19th centuries, and the relocated 1899 Don Train Station. Museum exhibitions (including beer-related stuff in the Brewery Gallery), seasonal events, an art center, and workshops add to the celebration of industry and entrepreneurship. One of Toronto's oldest community theater groups, the **East Side Players** (416-425-0917), performs four plays a year at Todmorden.

S E C R E T
BEES
⚜

During the summer months, take a self-directed stroll through the meadows at the **Kortright Centre for Conservation** (9550 Pine

Valley, Woodbridge, 905-832-2289), where bees do their business among the many flowers. A trail map is available from the visitors' center. Then drop in to the bee house (weekends only), where you can watch working hives from the safely screened-in viewing area, taste fresh honey... and learn the bee dance. During the annual Honey Festival, which usually falls on the second weekend of September, you can talk to professional beekeepers, watch cooking-with-honey demonstrations, make a beeswax candle, peruse the bee products for sale, and take guided nature tours.

The **Metropolitan Toronto Zoo** (Meadowvale Road, north of Highway 401, 416-392-5900) keeps a few working hives in the Eurasian walking area. Sometimes there's also a behavioral studies hive, where visitors can have an audience with the queen bee. (If you like bugs, you might also want to visit the zoo's butterfly garden or step inside to view the American and Malayan wood butterflies.) The zoo runs courses for serious beekeepers, as well as special-interest sessions for the public, usually in September. Call the education department (416-392-5947) to find out what's on.

If you've ever wondered how the sweet stuff gets from the hive to the honey jar, the **Billy Bee Honey Plant** (68 Tycos, 416-789-4391, ext. 0) offers free tours, including a couple of short films and a guided walk around the facility, for groups of 20 or more. Billy Bee is Canada's largest private honey packer, producing about 25 million pounds every year, and the plant has the latest honey processing and packaging equipment. Afterwards, poke your nose into **F.W. Jones and Sons** (68 Tycos, 416-783-2818), a beekeeping supply store right behind the plant, where you can get a close look at the specialized tools of the trade.

The **Ontario Beekeepers Association** (519-565-2622) hosts a honey competition in early November at the **Royal Winter Fair** (Coliseum,

Exhibition Place, 416-393-6418). Drop by the OBA booth, where you can buy honey, beeswax, bee pollen, and a sought-after skin cream, among other products. Professional beekeepers are on hand to talk to visitors, and there's a display of beekeeping equipment and an observation hive. Bees, of course, are not the only attraction. This is a full-fledged agricultural fair, with horse shows, dog trials, rodeo roping, and the popular "parade of cats." It's heaven for animal lovers.

SECRET
BELGIAN

Charming in an Old World kind of way, **Café Brussel** (124 Danforth, east of Broadview, 416-465-7363) is the place to go for mussels (almost 30 variations to choose from), Belgian beef beer stew, and baked chocolate mousse. It's the only authentic Belgian café in town, and a beer lover's paradise, with Stella Artois, Leffe Brune, Hoegaarden White, and Belle-Vue Kriek on tap and more Belgian varieties by the bottle, some unavailable elsewhere. There's also a very long wine list. Owner and chef Roger Stefan Wils, son of a Belgian chocolate maker, cooks up classic bistro fare with flair. After years in a tiny spot around the corner on Broadview, the café recently moved to bigger digs on the Danforth.

SECRET

BELLY DANCING

Dim lighting, cramped bench seats, and the faint essence of camel dung that emanates from the carpet-covered walls at **Sultan's Tent** (1280 Bay, second floor, 416-961-0601) all conspire to create the illusion of dining somewhere in the Moroccan desert (or Disneyland, depending on your willingness to suspend disbelief). Best of all, the belly dancing offers a welcome diversion from the prix-fixe dinner — couscous, overcooked lamb, and other predictable choices. There's no stage, so the dancers must negotiate the narrow aisles between tables, entrancing the crowd while dodging the waiters. Audience participation is encouraged, so choose your seat with care — park yourself close to the dance floor only if you're willing to reveal your sense of rhythm. Best enjoyed en masse, an evening at Sultan's Tent is perfect for special events, like birthday parties or Jack and Jill stags, where an element of tacky fun is not unwelcome.

Members of the Arabian Sahara Dance Company offer formally staged and sometimes narrated tales in the style of *The Arabian Nights* on Saturday nights at **Al Khaima Dining Theatre** (767 Dovercourt, 416-533-4849) — the name translates as "The Tent." Brass lamps, Moroccan carpets, and traditionally upholstered seating make a bid for cultural authenticity, while the menu offers both vegetarian and meat-based Arabic meals. Dinner theater tickets are available by reservation only, but after 10 p.m. the half-price general admission will get you a drink and the last of three shows.

SECRET
BIBLIOPHILISM

If the smell of old books puts you in a nostalgic mood, you'll enjoy the **Old Paper Show and Sale** (St. Lawrence North Market, 92 Front East, 416-410-1310), which sets up shop twice a year, usually on a Sunday in late March and again in October. Call to find out exact dates, and prepare to rummage through bins and box loads of old postcards, calendars, used books and first editions, collectibles, and endless aisles of ephemera.

The **Thomas Fisher Rare Book Library** (120 St. George, at Harbord, 416-978-5285), a noncirculating, closed-stack library at the University of Toronto, is one of the city's true treasures. The varied collection, ranging from a Babylonian cuneiform tablet from 1789 BC to original drafts and printed works of contemporary Canadian writers, reflects the diversity of research conducted at the university. Among the many holdings: Henry Scadding's *Codex Torontonensis*, an 11th-century Greek text of the four Gospels; a copy of Johannes Balbus's *Catholicon*, printed in the 1460s, possibly by Johannes Gutenberg; 20 letters that Florence Nightingale wrote between 1873 and 1879 to her friend and pupil, Annie Machin; the Birdsall Bookbinding Collection of 3,000 finishing tools from the firm of Birdsall & Son of Northampton, England, and bindings produced by the firm; and a collection of more than 1,000 broadsides, pamphlets, and books from the Canadian typographic firm of Cooper and Beatty. The library mounts regular exhibitions, and Friends of the Thomas Fisher Rare Book Library sponsor an annual series of guest speakers.

If you love books for their look and feel, you may be enticed by the opportunity to make them yourself. The **Canadian Bookbinders and Book Artists Guild** (416-581-1071) teaches both bookbinding basics and specialized skills, such as wooden-board binding, metal-working techniques for creating ornamental clasps, leather work, and letterpress printing. Class locations vary — call for a complete schedule.

S E C R E T
BIRDS

More than 250 bird species have been spotted on the Leslie Street Spit, a five-kilometer (three-mile) peninsula poking into Lake Ontario. Created in the 1950s as a landfill site, the rubble soon sprouted greenery and has since been designated an environmentally protected area. Renamed **Tommy Thomson Park** (foot of Leslie, south of Lakeshore Boulevard East, 416-661-6600), the spit is home to one of the world's largest colonies of ring-billed gulls — 40,000 or 50,000 nesting pairs — as well as black-crowned night herons, double-crested cormorants, and others. There's no admission fee, and during the summer the TTC runs a free weekend shuttle bus along the spit.

Like other migratory birds, hawks head south for the winter. But rather than take the shortest route, hawks prefer to fly around, rather than over, large bodies of water. Consequently, as they head south in the fall, they tend to congregate along the north shores of the Great Lakes, and one popular route leads directly over Toronto. During the annual migration period, from September 1 to November 30, raptor fans and official hawk watchers gather for the **High Park Hawk**

Watch, meeting on a little knoll just north of the Grenadier Restaurant parking lot (High Park, Bloor Street entrance). The hawks are plentiful — literally thousands of southbound birds pass over during the three-month vigil — and even a few golden eagles have been known to cruise by. The **Greater Toronto Raptor Watch** (www.gtrw.ca) and the **Toronto Ornithological Club** organize the hawk monitoring. An official volunteer "counter," skilled in the art of field identification, comes to the viewing area every day, along with other volunteer watchers. Interested birders are always welcome. If you're wondering why the same ritual doesn't take place again in the spring, it's because our feathered friends prefer to take a different route when they're homeward bound, following the Niagara Peninsula between Lake Ontario and Lake Erie and continuing north along the Bruce Peninsula.

A good location for year-round bird watching is the 300-acre **Humber Arboretum** (from Highway 27, turn west onto Humber College Boulevard, then south on Arboretum, 416-675-5009). More than 100 species have been sighted, including numerous meadow birds, upwards of a dozen warblers, several raptors (great horned owls and red-shouldered hawks among them), and water birds like herons and green-winged teals.

Expert-led field trips to birding hot spots around the province, as well as in-town presentations by exceptional North American birders, are organized by the **Ontario Field Ornithologists** (Box 455, Station R, Toronto, ON, M4G 4E1, www.interlog.com/~ofo). The OFO also publishes small, inexpensive site guides, with a map and area highlights. They're available on request, but you should allow time for mailing.

The **Toronto Ornithological Club** organizes a dozen or more Toronto walks every year, mostly in May and September, to destinations, including the Leslie Street Spit, the Toronto Islands, and

Humber Bay. These and other activities are announced on the **Rare Bird Hotline** (416-350-3000, ext. 2293) a week or so ahead of time. Even if nothing's afoot, it's fun to call the hot line for a recorded report about recent sightings of rare feathered species.

If you'd prefer to watch the birds in the comfort of your own backyard, you can attract them with feeders, bird baths, and a supply of birdseed from the **Canadian Wild Bird Company** (622 Mount Pleasant, between Davisville and Eglinton, 416-484-4080) or **Birders Nature Store** (265 Eglinton West, 416-481-2431). An admirable selection of guidebooks can be found at **Open Air Books and Maps** (25 Toronto Street, corner of Adelaide, 416-363-0719). Of course, good optics are essential — for professional-quality binoculars and telescopes, check out the stores listed under "Secret Astronomy."

If you prefer watching birds that stay absolutely still, visit the **Royal Ontario Museum** (100 Queen's Park, 416-586-5551), where hundreds of stuffed bird specimens, including an albatross with a nine-foot wingspan, are artfully displayed in various museum mounts and dioramas. No binoculars required. For cyber-ornithologists, the ROM has created an **online field guide to Ontario birds** (www.rom. on.ca/ontario/fieldguides.html) that provides descriptions, pictures, and audio samples for more than 50 of the most common summer bird species in Metropolitan Toronto. Other areas of the ROM Web site include a birdsong quiz and a detailed study of the tragically extinct great auk — the ROM owns a specimen, but it is locked away in a vault for serious study only.

The medieval art of falconry is alive and flapping at the **Falconry Centre** (near Tottenham, on the first road north of Highway 9, between the town line and Tottenham Road, 905-936-1033), a unique educational breeding farm boasting more than 200 birds of prey.

Walk among trained eagles, falcons, hawks, and owls, observe babies in the breeding aviaries, visit the educational displays, and watch daily flying demonstrations. These birds are truly awe inspiring, and this is a rare opportunity to see them at close range. The center is open from Victoria Day weekend through Labor Day weekend.

If you were asked to name the fastest animal on earth, you'd probably say the cheetah. Anyone who grew up watching Mutual of Omaha's *Wild Kingdom*, with mustachioed host Marlin Perkins, knows these spotted cats can achieve speeds of 128 km/h (80 mph). But in fact, the fastest animal is the peregrine falcon. When this hunting bird tucks in its wings and goes into a stoop, or straight-down dive, it can hit the 320-km/h (200-mph) mark. In the 1950s, the peregrine population took a sudden nosedive. Within 20 years, the species was almost extinct, due to widespread use of the pesticide DDT. These magnificent birds are now making a comeback, and in 1995 a pair of peregrines arrived in downtown Toronto, becoming the first pair to nest successfully in southern Ontario in over 30 years. The **Canadian Peregrine Foundation** (416-481-1233, www.peregrine-foundation.ca) is a dedicated group of volunteers who rescue fallen fledglings and document the recovery of the peregrine falcon and other raptors at risk across Canada. They've set up several Web cams, including one in Toronto, to watch over the nests, and they maintain a log of peregrine sightings. The foundation raises money by selling memberships and gifts, including T-shirts, jigsaw puzzles, and mouse pads. You can also adopt a peregrine, which entitles you to a lovely photo certificate, a newsletter subscription, and a year-end update letting you know what your chosen bird has been up to.

SECRET
BOATS

Permanently docked at Ontario Place, the HMCS *Haida* (955 Lakeshore Boulevard West, 416-314-9755) is one of only two remaining ships sailed by the Royal Canadian Navy (RCN) in World War II — several hundred others were either sunk or scrapped — and the last remaining Tribal Class destroyer in the world. *Haida* achieved fame while helping a mixed force of British, Canadian, and Polish warships clear enemy shipping off the coast of France in anticipation of the 1944 D-Day landings. During this period, *Haida* destroyed more enemy vessels than any other ship in the RCN. The gray behemoth functions now as a training site for sea cadets and as a naval museum (open daily from mid-May to Labor Day and weekends until mid-October).

Another big boat parked in the harbor is **Captain John's** (1 Queen's Quay West, at the foot of Yonge, 416-363-6062), a floating seafood restaurant and banquet hall. Apparently, this monument to kitsch was once a pleasure cruiser in the private fleet of Tito, former president of Yugoslavia. Since the 1970s, however, proprietor John Lesnik (who lives onboard) has faithfully donned his fake captain's uniform and presided over so-so dinners of shark and lobster. Permission to come aboard, sir?

A converted 1920s shipping warehouse is home to **The Pier: Toronto's Waterfront Museum** (245 Queen's Quay West, between York and Spadina, 416-338-7437). Special exhibits, videos, and interactive displays reveal the history of Toronto harbor and the Great Lakes. Clamber aboard the refurbished 1932 steam tug *Ned Hanlan*, take a walking tour of the waterfront, or rent a heritage boat and explore the harbor on your own.

The **Royal Canadian Yacht Club Archives** (141 St. George, 416-967-7245) preserve evidence of marine history from 1850 to the present, including the club records, artworks in oil and watercolor, a collection of models, and a nautical library. If you're interested in visiting, call ahead to make sure the archivist is on duty.

SECRET

BODY ART

Stainless Studios Body Art (609 Queen West, just east of Bathurst, 416-504-1433) has a reputation for poking holes in all the right places. For decoration and primitive pleasure, they offer custom-made jewelry, from nails and nipple tusks to frenum loops and prince's wands. They do tattoos too. Owner Tom Brazda, who takes a service industry approach, calls himself "one part counselor, one part doctor, and one part technician." The studio itself, with its skylights and spiral staircase, avoids the hospital look in favor of apartment-style comfort.

Custom body design by the in-house and guest artists at **Urban Primitive** (216 Carlton, just west of Parliament, 416-966-9155) involves both modern and hand-tattooing methods, as well as a variety of flesh intervention techniques, from branding and piercing to scarification. Body painting, permanent makeup, and traditional and contemporary mehendi (henna designs) are also available. The Urban Primitive philosophy is rooted in pre-Christian paganism and influenced by tribal beliefs in the ritual and healing aspects of body modification.

Passage Body Piercing (473 Church, at Wellesley, 416-929-7330) offers discreet assistance with "all your exotic piercing needs." You'll know what those are, better than I do, so enough said.

There are many shops in Toronto where you can get your body inked. For intricate, custom artwork, check out the colorful creations at **Way Cool Tattoos** (679 Queen West, 416-603-0145), **King of Fools** (556 Church, 416-323-8777), and **Reactive Ink** (283 Augusta, in Kensington Market, 416-204-1657). Wherever you choose to get decorated, insist on hygienic methods, including properly scrubbed and sterilized instruments, new needles, and a freshly gloved tattoo artist.

S E C R E T
BONSAI

It began in China more than a thousand years ago, but the art of bonsai was truly developed by the Japanese. The name itself is a Japanese word meaning "tray-planted," and it refers to the art of training and growing miniature trees in containers. Skillful artists control the growth by gently wiring the trunk and branches, then pruning and shaping them to suggest much larger trees, standing upright in a field or weathered and bent with age. The beauty of a natural landscape is evoked in the viewer's imagination. Every Sunday when the weather's warm, the **Bonsai Man** pulls his van into the parking lot at the corner of Bathurst and Davenport, next to Starkman Surgical Supply (1243 Bathurst), and sets up a small forest of the imagination. Fifty or 60 tiny, well-trimmed trees are displayed on makeshift tables or inside and on top of his van. Prices range from $25 to over $200, depending on size and style, and every tree comes with good advice for taking care of it — but no guarantee.

Since 1963, the **Toronto Bonsai Society** (416-661-0620) has been promoting the horticultural techniques and artistic principles of this ancient art. One of the largest clubs outside Japan, the society holds regular monthly meetings, where beginners can learn bonsai techniques. At least once a year, the society invites an international bonsai master to give a series of lectures, demonstrations, and workshops. Members can buy basic supplies, such as wire and bonsai tools, and take advantage of group orders of pots and other paraphernalia directly from Japan. Membership costs a mere $35 a year, and meetings are held at the **Civic Garden Centre** (777 Lawrence East, at Leslie) on the second Monday of every month except July and August, when informal weekly workshops are arranged in members' gardens.

SECRET
BOOKSTORES

To describe all of Toronto's independent, used, alternative, and chain bookstores would require an entire book in itself. Luckily, such a book already exists: *A Guide to the Bookstores of Toronto*, by Arthur Wenk and Peggy Warren-Wenk (ECW Press). It's a little dated now but still a good introduction to this city's wealth of reading emporiums. Elsewhere in *Secret Toronto*, specialty bookstores are listed under relevant headings — check the index for a complete list. Below are a few independent bookstores that deserve to be singled out.

Toronto's best independent mini-chain is **Book City**, whose flagship store (501 Bloor West, between Bathurst and Spadina, 416-961-4496) anchors the trendy Annex neighborhood. All new hardcovers are immediately discounted by 10 percent, the prices are always low on stacks of remaindered books, and the stores stay open late seven days a week (other locations: 2530 Bloor West, 416-766-9412; 348 Danforth, 416-469-9997; 1950 Queen East, 416-698-1444).

Founded by community activist Wesley Crichlow, **A Different Booklist** (746 Bathurst, south of Bloor, 416-538-0889) stocks culturally diverse literature — identity-affirming voices and visions from black, First Nations, Latin and South American, Asian, lesbian and gay, and feminist authors. Browse the shelves or drop by for monthly events, from readings and book launches to receptions, workshops, screenings, and even live theater.

Another Story (164 Danforth, east of Broadview, 416-462-1104) specializes in alternative views on contemporary social issues. Lining the shelves are books about labor and Native issues, antiracist litera-ture, feminist works, gay and lesbian titles, and nonsexist children's books that emphasize other cultures. A strong selection of related magazines is also available.

In business for more than a quarter century, **Glad Day Bookshop** (598A Yonge, 416-961-4161) is Toronto's only specifically lesbian and gay bookstore. More than 6,000 fiction and nonfiction titles are in stock — despite regular interference by self-appointed censors at Canada Customs.

This Ain't the Rosedale Library (483 Church, at Maitland, 416-929-9912), which also carries a strong selection of gay and lesbian titles, specializes in new fiction and baseball books. Discounts and high-quality remainders serve bargain hunters well, and browsers are treated to a face-out display for most covers. This store is a haven for committed readers.

Books by and about women are the focus at the **Toronto Women's Bookstore** (73 Harbord, near Spadina, 416-922-8744), which also serves as a networking center for the feminist and lesbian communities. Employees arrange readings and workshops, a bulletin board displays community information, and there's a health and counseling referral service for women. Now the largest nonprofit feminist bookstore in Canada, it started out 30 years ago as a single shelf of books in a resource center.

You can enjoy the pleasures of an old-style bookstore at **Nicholas Hoare** (45 Front East, 416-777-2665), a not-so-old shop occupying a renovated building in Toronto's theater district, with wooden floors, brass railings, and armchairs for reading or resting in front of the fireplace. The collection favors 20th-century literature, children's books, and art books thoughtfully displayed face out.

SECRET
BREAKFAST

Favored by musicians and film industry types who don't like to spoil the morning by getting out of bed too early, the minuscule **Mimi's Restaurant** (218 Bathurst, north of Queen, 416-703-6464) serves amazing all-day breakfasts. Seating is restricted to half a dozen stools at the counter and a handful of cozy booths, decorated with plastic toys and *Star Trek* memorabilia, and the service can sometimes be surly, but the homemade chili and scrambled-egg concoctions are ample compensation. Mimi's is easy to find if you look for the large yellow Oak Leaf Steam Baths sign — the restaurant is right beneath.

East-enders enjoy **Hello Toast** (993 Queen East, east of Pape, 416-778-7299), known for its weekend brunch and fabulous French toast. The retro dining-room furniture and funky fiberglass chandelier set the scene for eggs Benedict with smoked salmon, omelette specials, and other breakfasts accompanied by slices of multigrain or buttered challah.

While the Little Italy section of College Street is predominantly an evening or afternoon destination, greasy-spoon breakfast fare can be enjoyed closer to Bathurst at **Mars** (432 College, 416-921-6332) and the nearby **Kos Bar and Grill** (434 College, 416-923-1868).

The classic Queen Street equivalent is the **Stem Open Kitchen** (354 Queen West, east of Spadina, 416-593-0530), run by the same gentle folks who've had it since the '60s. Long and narrow, there's just enough room for the waitress to sidle up and down between the booths and counter stools.

People go out of their way to enjoy the huge, diner-style breakfasts at **Sunset Grill** (2006 Queen East, 416-690-9985), opposite Kew Gardens in the Beaches. For those who wake up very, very late, the restaurant serves breakfast 24 hours a day.

The **Gem Bar and Grill** (1159 Davenport, west of Ossington, 416-654-1182) is another neighborhood favorite, complete with neon and jukebox atmosphere. Meanwhile, the **Only Café** (972 Danforth, near Donlands, 416-463-7843) is the only place to order a Cowgirl's Breakfast or a Guy de Maupassant sandwich. The menu also includes Belgian waffles replete with eight varieties of fruit, plus whipped cream and dark chocolate. Beer for breakfast may or may not appeal, but the Only Café has such a long list of ales (97 at last count) that you might be tempted to linger until the afternoon or evening.

The delicious, delicate lobster-and-cheese Bretonne is only one of more than a dozen omelettes on the menu at **Jacques Bistro du Parc** (126 Cumberland, 416-961-1893). This narrow second-floor spot, overlooking the Village of Yorkville Park (see "Secret Parks"), serves French bistro fare worthy of Paris.

S E C R E T
BRUNCH

Off the beaten track but well worth the detour, **Mitzi's Café and Gallery** (100 Sorauren, at Pearson, 416-588-1234) serves homemade pizzas that change according to market conditions (supermarket, not stock market). There are also BLTs with roasted garlic, vegetarian sandwiches, and a changing assortment of daily specials. The decor is eclectic, to say the least, but comfortable in a funky farm-kitchen kind of way.

It's hard to tell whether the downmarket decor — worn '70s-style couches, Arborite tables with mismatched chairs, an unhinged shower-stall door — was found in the basement or bought from one of Toronto's many purveyors of period furniture. But the overall effect at **Aunties and Uncles** (74 Lippincott, at College, 416-324-1375) is one of hip, casual decay. Don't let it worry you, though, because the food is fresh. Open only until 4 p.m., every day but Monday, this neighborhood hangout serves strong coffee, daily soups like cold carrot and leek, tasty clubhouse sandwiches on thick-sliced challah,

Belgian waffles, omelettes, and eggs fried to order. The rooms are small and funky, including a second-floor retreat. In good weather, the street-side patio with its picnic tables and white-picket fence is a popular spot to regenerate after a late night in the clubs.

Chow down on blintzes every Sunday at **Free Times Café** (320 College, 416-967-1078). From 11 a.m. to 3 p.m., Toronto's oldest folk club lays out an authentic all-you-can-eat Jewish buffet, featuring potato latkes, eggs with lox and onions, pickled herring, gefilte fish, French toast made with challah, salmon patties, cabbage salad, bagels, lox and cream cheese, and plenty of sweets. The traditional cooking, revived by owner Judy Perly from old cookbooks and favorite family recipes, is accompanied by live Yiddish and Klezmer music (two sets, at noon and 1:20 p.m.). Arrive early or make a reservation, because the Free Times fills up quickly. Regular brunch, with the usual omelettes, frittatas, and bagels, is available on Saturday but without the live music, alas.

If you head out to Leslieville for a little retro-furniture shopping (see "Secret Antiques"), you can fuel up on weekend brunch at **Verveine** (1097 Queen East, 416-405-9906). Try the walnut-crusted French toast with poached pears and Stilton stuffing or the poached eggs on a croissant. Come back at dinnertime for whole roasted snapper or Chilean sea bass and a flourish of homemade desserts. Verveine is right next to **Kristapson's** (1095 Queen East, 416-466-5152), which has been making Toronto's best smoked salmon since 1953. The tiny shop sells little else, and its single-minded devotion is evident in the many "best of" awards decorating the walls.

Naturally, smoked salmon turns up on the menu at Verveine, as well as at **Bonjour Brioche** (812 Queen East, 416-406-1250), several blocks west. The weekend brunch includes scrambled eggs with smoked salmon, sour cream, chives, and caviar, an omelette Provençal with black olives, rosemary, and Gruyère, and other specials, accompanied by a section of fresh, chewy baguettes. Bonjour Brioche is best known for its breads and baked goods, favored by many TO restaurateurs.

SECRET

BUBBLE TEA

Originating as a teen craze in Taiwan, bubble tea popped up on Asian menus around town a couple of years ago and has even inspired entire cafés devoted to this unusual drink. Sometimes called pearl milk tea or boba ice tea, it usually consists of iced tea and milk with a cluster of dark, squishy tapioca balls — the bubbles. Flavors are all over the map, from peppermint, peach, and peanut to chocolate, honey dew, and mung bean. The drink is served with a jumbo-sized straw (for sucking up the bubbles) in a large glass, much like a milkshake. **Love and Scandal** (120 Cumberland, second floor, 416-964-0302), in Toronto's upscale Yorkville district, offers 101 varieties of bubble tea, from strawberry to garlic, as well as 14 flavors of toast — best enjoyed while listening to Korean pop ballads and watching the bubble-shaped TV. The name of this café comes from a Henry Fielding quote: "Love and scandal are the best sweeteners of tea." Bubble tea drinkers also congregate at **Tea Shop 168** (419 College, 416-603-9168). Several varieties of the bumpy stuff are on the menu at **Spring Rolls on Yonge** (693 Yonge, 416-972-7655), along with decent pad thai, tom yum kai soup, and Vietnamese pho (beef stock soup). For the complete experience, head to Markham, where you'll find two **Tea Shop 168** outlets (905-479-6168 and 905-940-9168) in the sprawling **Pacific Mall** (4300 Steeles East, at Kennedy), a glitzy monument to Hong Kong culture.

S E C R E T

BURGERS

Rosemary is the secret ingredient in the moist burgers at **Utopia Café and Grill** (585 College, 416-534-7751), an unpretentious little spot just east of Clinton, generally overlooked by those heading to the many hipper hangouts along this boomtown stretch of College. Extravagant toppings like grilled eggplant and roasted garlic are standard at **Groucho's Gourmet Burgers** (1574 Bayview, 416-482-3456). More important, the grilling of the key ingredient — the burger itself — is excellent. The downstairs restaurant at **The Senator** (249 Victoria, 416-364-7517) has great gourmet burgers during the day, and the upscale atmosphere is a bit of a departure from the usual burger joint decor.

S E C R E T

CAFÉS

A cuppa java isn't hard to come by in Toronto — 20 paces in any direction will bring you to the doorstep of one coffee chain or another, whether it's a Second Cup (a Toronto original), a Starbucks, a Timothy's, or a European-style Lettieri. But the best spots for atmosphere and service with personality are one-off cafés. (See also "Secret Coffee Beans.")

Little Italy is Toronto's hot spot for the hip and cool, and good espresso comes naturally at **Bar Italia** (582 College, east of Clinton, 416-535-3621). Favorites from the kitchen include salmon on a salad of arugula, new potatoes, and endive and the Cubano sandwich (warm pork with garlic mayonnaise and avocado). Set back slightly from the sidewalk, Bar Italia has room for a few outdoor tables, suitable for summertime street-watching. The supreme spot for surveying the passing College Street crowd, however, is still the outdoor patio at **Café Diplomatico** (594 College, 416-534-4637), where the coffee is mediocre but the service is friendly and the ambience sublimely relaxed. Extending the full length of the café and facing west onto Clinton, the patio is perfectly placed for afternoon sunshine — even in winter, you risk getting a suntan when you're sitting inside next to the bright, west-side windows. Farther along on College Street, just a little off the beaten latte track, **Il Gatto Nero** (656 College, 416-536-3132) serves excellent espresso.

Faema Coffee Machines (672 Dupont, at Christie, 416-535-1555) is best known as the purveyor of fine Italian espresso makers. Indeed, don't forget to browse their upstairs showroom for the latest in steamers, either before or after enjoying a beverage from the main-floor espresso bar. Sit on a stool at one of the high marble-topped tables, sample a slice of honey-drizzled walnut cake, and gaze out through the plate glass at passing traffic from the nearby Loblaws supermarché.

Finding **Luna** (181 Dovercourt, north of Queen, 416-588-3374) feels like a lucky accident — even if you've been here before. Once a corner variety store, kitty-corner to a Catholic church, this seren-dipitous site on a residential street retains a retro atmosphere. With excellent espresso and a small sidewalk patio, Luna makes me want to move into the neighborhood so I can bring the morning paper here more often.

Despite the influx of coffee chains and other contenders — at least a dozen cafés now grace the trendy Queen East strip between Wood-bine and Victoria Park — the **Roastery** (2018 Queen East, 416-698-5090) is still a Beaches neighborhood favorite, with its eclectic decor and unbeatable location directly across from Kew Gardens. Nearby, the dark-walled **Remarkable Bean** (2242 Queen East, 416-690-2420) offers a refuge for cinephiles (coming out of the Fox cinema) and chess players alike. Also remarkable at the Bean are the fabulous, fragrant loose herbal and fruit teas, like the mango-strawberry blend. If you lean toward chic, try **Mersini** (2120 Queen East, at Hammersmith, 416-699-9444), where Mediterranean appetizers and a full range of coffees are available late — till 3 a.m. on Friday and Saturday.

Out in Parkdale, just west of the overhead train bridge at Dufferin, the **Rustic Cosmo Café** (1278 Queen West, 416-531-4924) is imme-diately inviting, with warm wood and brick, high ceilings, and home baking. Local artwork and a couple of jewelry displays — not to mention the presence of the artists themselves, sipping coffee and living the life — reflect the area's alternative community. Loft dwell-ers who once inhabited Queen Street closer to Spadina have been pushed farther and farther west by rising rents and commercial gentrification. Parkdale has become the latest refuge and last best hope for the unwealthy creative crowd — it will be a very long time (touch wood) before The Gap opens a store in this neighborhood.

S E C R E T
CAKES

The cranberry pecan pie from **Desserts by Phipps** (420 Eglinton West, west of Avenue Road, 416-481-9111) has become a holiday staple in our house. Even after stuffing myself with turkey and trimmings, I can't say no to a slice. But you don't have to wait for the holidays to celebrate — cake is always in season. Phipps creates at least 25 different desserts, displaying a particular affection for chocolate. Although they supply cafés and restaurants around town, the outlet on Eglinton has a handful of tables, where you can indulge yourself at the source.

Back in 1975, after a stint baking desserts for the Cow Café, Dufflet Rosenberg started her own home business. Her sweet genius inspired a company that now delivers more than 100 different cakes and pastries to more than 350 restaurants and cafés. If you're perusing an after-dinner lineup of desserts at some restaurant counter, look for Dufflet's trademark cardboard cake circle with concentric black and white rings (sometimes covered with a doily) sitting underneath each baked creation. The tiny retail outlet for **Dufflet Pastries** (787 Queen West, three blocks west of Bathurst, 416-504-2870) carries a small daily selection of sweet stuff, as well as pizza, vegetarian soups, and fresh roasted coffee from the Green Bean Roastery in Oakville. Dufflet Rosenberg's signature cakes and tortes include cappuccino dacquoise, chocolate raspberry truffle, and lemon strawberry mousse. Special orders placed before 3 p.m. can be picked up at the store after noon the following day. If you're out for a stroll in the wee hours near Queen and Dovercourt, walk past the glass-walled cake factory, located just south of Queen where Dovercourt turns into Sudbury

Street, and catch a glimpse of the bakers going about their all-night business.

Pointy, pyramid-shaped desserts can be consumed in casual surroundings at the **Pyramid Cakery** (2519 Yonge, four blocks north of Eglinton, 416-489-2246), where wooden tables and small lamps lend a parlor atmosphere. The light menu also includes soup and sandwiches (the avocado and crab is a favorite).

Belgian chocolate, butter, and cream are the reigning triumvirate at **Rahier Patisserie** (1717 Bayview, south of Eglinton, 416-482-0917), where owners Sonia and François Rahier craft cakes and tarts to die for. There are two small tables, in case you just can't make it out the door before treating yourself to a taste of heaven.

SECRET
CANADIANA

Downtown crowds busily shopping at The Bay may not be aware of the Canadian art collection hanging in a little-known gallery directly overhead. The permanent display at the **Thomson Gallery** (176 Yonge, at Queen, ninth floor, 416-861-4571), owned by newspaper magnate Ken Thomson, includes canvases by Emily Carr, Tom Thomson, and Group of Seven artists, such as Lawren Harris and J.E.H. MacDonald. Also on show are several of Cornelius Krieghoff's habitant paintings and works by less famous artists, such as William Berczy and explorer Paul Kane.

SECRET
CARPETS

From its origins in the 1970s as a small private collection of carpets, the **Museum for Textiles** (55 Centre, one block east of University and Dundas, 416-599-5515) has been spun into a major center for the study and exhibition of ornamental and wearable textiles. More than 16,000 carpets, tapestries, garments, ceremonial cloths, and related artifacts are now preserved in the museum's collection. The Canadiana display of hooked rugs and quilts is particularly strong, although the holdings extend to Indonesian, Central and South Asian, and South American textiles. The museum comprises about a dozen gallery spaces under one roof, including a contemporary gallery that shows current work by fiber artists.

Well-heeled rug shoppers are advised to visit **Elte Carpets and Home** (80 Ronald, northeast of Dufferin and Eglinton West, 416-785-7885), a cavernous warehouse with a wide range of beautiful imports. Anyone with an affection for John F. and Jackie Kennedy will be thrilled to know that they can now own a replica of a floral Victorian carpet that resided in the Oval Office during the Kennedy era. The original rug was purchased by American manufacturer Nourisan for US$43,000 at the Kennedy memorabilia auction, and Elte is the sole Canadian distributor of carpets reproduced from the parent piece. Floor coverings aren't the only reason to visit Elte — the furniture emporium carries leathery Ralph Lauren chairs and sofas (among other stuff), there's a little onsite faux '50s diner, and **Summerhill Decorative Hardware** (80 Ronald, 416-785-1225) shares the same roof. Nearby, **Ginger's International Bath Centre**

(1275 Castlefield, 416-787-1787) offers upscale fittings, including a Philippe Starck stainless steel sink, plus mirrors, soap dishes, and such.

S E C R E T
CEMETERIES

Felix Oswald, the twisted protagonist of Toronto writer Graeme Gibson's 1971 novel *Communion*, eats his lunch every day on a stone cemetery bench. He sits dead center between two beautiful, half-naked women (carved from Laurentian pink granite at opposite ends of the bench), before turning his amorous attention to one or the other. The monument Gibson describes — belonging to Toronto businessman Lionel Cutten, his wife Annie Rowena Cutten, and her sister, Helen Gertrude Moncur — was carved in 1936 by German-born sculptor Emanuel Hahn for the Cutten plot in **Mount Pleasant Cemetery** (375 Mount Pleasant, 416-485-9129). Hahn contributed other, perhaps more prominent works to Toronto, including the large bronze statue of Adam Beck located on University Avenue, south of Queen, and the oar-wielding likeness of rower Ned Hanlan on the grounds of the Canadian National Exhibition.

The Cutten memorial is located just north of the mausoleum and crematorium chapel and not far from the columns and Corinthian capitals of the stately Eaton mausoleum, where department-store founder Timothy Eaton and at least 15 family members are interred. Most of the carved granite for this memorial, erected by block and tackle in the early 1900s, was imported from Scotland — not for pomp but because Canada's granite industry was undeveloped, and it was impossible to make polished columns here at the time.

Indeed, walking from west to east in Mount Pleasant Cemetery, one can trace the evolution of the monument industry and changing fashions in stone markers, as well as the changing face of Toronto society. Columns and Celtic crosses near Yonge Street turn to military memorials, Masonic symbols, and increasing floral ornamentation, then give way to the multicultural mosaic east of Mount Pleasant Road, where Ukrainian wheat stalks and Polish eagles blend with Chinese pagodas and painted Vietnamese inscriptions.

Opened in 1876, Mount Pleasant Cemetery was laid out by landscape designer Henry Engelhardt, who transformed a 200-acre farm into elegant parkland, complete with a small lake and first-class arboretum expressly created for public enjoyment. Mount Pleasant now contains more than 168,000 burial sites, including many belonging to Toronto's founders, politicians, and prominent business owners. A pamphlet available from the main office (located just east of Mount Pleasant Road, open weekdays only) provides a guided history tour of more than 50 famous plots, including those of insulin discoverers Frederick Banting and Charles Best (buried separately, though not far from one another), former prime minister William Lyon Mackenzie King, pianist Glenn Gould, Maple Leaf hockey great Charlie Conacher, and Dr. Jennie Smillie Robertson, Canada's first female surgeon and cofounder of the original Women's College Hospital in 1911, as well as a monument to the ill-fated *Empress of Ireland* (see "Secret Salvation"). The cemetery gates are open from 8 a.m. to dusk (about 8:30 p.m. in summer and 5 p.m. in winter).

Developers digging up the ground in 1956 for a new Scarborough subdivision discovered an Iroquois burial site, a mound containing the remains of almost 500 early inhabitants. Bones from the mass

grave, dating back to 1250 AD, were ceremonially reburied during a Great Feast of the Dead. The **Taber Hill Ossuaries** (Taber Hill Park, on Bellamy, north of Lawrence), as the site is now called, were marked by a very large boulder bearing a small plaque, perched on top of the re-covered mound. Taber Hill Park is tiny and the memorial unassuming, although the names of nearby Indian Mound Crescent and Six Nations Avenue serve as additional reminders. History buffs can learn more about the site by visiting the nearby **Scarborough Board of Education Archives** (730 Golf Club, north of Lawrence, 416-396-6930), which keep a vertical file of press clippings and other documents. The archives are open on Thursday only, from 7 p.m. to 9 p.m., or by appointment.

SECRET
CERAMICS

Often overlooked in favor of the much grander Royal Ontario Museum (ROM) across the street, the **Gardiner Museum of Ceramic Art** (111 Queen's Park, just south of Bloor, 416-586-8080) is well worth a visit. The internationally renowned collection ranges from ancient pre-Columbian ritual vessels, through Renaissance Italian tin-glazed earthenware, 17th-century posset pots and fuddling cups from English taverns, commedia dell'arte figures, and yellow porcelain from the Age of Enlightenment, to contemporary works from around the world. Regular traveling exhibits round out the display. Ask about the lectures and educational programs, or visit the Clay Pit to try your hand at the craft, with guidance from professional potters. If you'd rather just drink from a cup, without having to make it first,

then reserve a spot on the Tuesday tour and afternoon tea (2 p.m. to
4 p.m., $5 for tea). Admission to the gallery is only a few dollars or
free with a stub from the ROM.

The **Clay Room** (279 Danforth, Chester or Pape subway, 416-466-
8474) offers do-it-yourself ceramics, where you skip the potting and
go straight to the painting. The store has more than 75 different
mugs, bowls, and other unfinished items to choose from. You pay for
the pot (or whatever), plus an hourly fee — painting supplies are
included.

The **Harbourfront Craft Studio** (Harbourfront Centre, 235 Queen's
Quay West, 416-973-4963) offers ongoing introductory craft courses,
including potting, silk-screen printing, glass blowing, and metal
jewelry making, taught by resident artisans. Informal studio tours take
place every Sunday, or you can stroll through the viewing gallery any
day of the week and watch the proceedings. **Bounty**, the craft shop
across the hall, sells work produced onsite.

The **Guild Shop** (118 Cumberland, 416-921-1721) has been show-
casing the work of Ontario artisans since 1932, when it was managed
by the Canadian Guild of Crafts. In 1976, the guild merged with the
Ontario Craft Foundation to form the Ontario Crafts Council, which
now oversees the Yorkville store. Here, they sell exquisitely handcrafted ceramics, as well as jewelry, textiles, hand-blown glass, and
wood objects. The store also mounts exhibitions of Inuit and First
Nations art. The Ontario Crafts Council, a not-for-profit service
organization that promotes craft, also runs the **Craft Gallery** and the
Ontario Crafts Council Resource Centre (Designer's Walk, 170
Bedford Street, Suite 300, 416-925-4222, ext. 229), where you'll find
an extensive collection of national and international publications, a
slide-rental library, a portfolio registry of more than 300 craftspeople,
and an exhibition gallery.

SECRET
CHEFS-IN-TRAINING

George Brown College runs this country's largest hospitality training school, where aspiring chefs learn to make superior sauces — local chef-celeb Jamie Kennedy, for example, is a George Brown grad. Cooks in training need people to practice on, so the school kitchen opened its doors to the public and launched **Siegfried's Dining Room** (300 Adelaide East, 416-415-2260), named in honor of distinguished professor Siegfried Bulla. The restaurant is open on weekdays only, from September to May. The prix-fixe menu changes daily, and naturally it's cheaper at lunch than at dinner, but the food is far superior to any other school's cafeteria grub. After all, these students intend to be more than just short-order cooks, and the proof is literally in the pudding.

SECRET
CHICKEN LIVERS

After marinating in tequila, lime, and cayenne, the chicken livers are blackened at **Southern Accent** (595 Markham, south of Bloor, 416-536-3211), in the style unique to Cajun cooking. This is one of the best places in town for spicy gumbo, hush puppies (tender fried cornmeal appetizers), jambalaya, and other southern gems.

At **Pan** (516 Danforth, 416-466-8158), the little organs are given the Greek treatment. Pan is also a great place on the Danforth to take a break from souvlaki — try the lamb with fig sauce or the crusted sea bass.

SECRET
CHILDHOOD

Among the many treasures in the **Osborne Collection of Early Children's Books** (Lillian H. Smith Public Library, 239 College, 416-393-7753), visitors can view a 14th-century manuscript of Aesop's famous fables, school texts from the 16th century, Victorian classics, and even childhood books belonging to Florence Nightingale. The Smith library itself is a delightful building to visit, with its colorful patterned brickwork, castle-like aura, and iron griffins arched at the doorway. Beyond the Osborne archive, the library also houses an extensive contemporary children's literature collection, the Merril Collection of Science Fiction, Speculation and Fantasy (named for the late SF writer Judith Merril, who spent much of her life in Toronto), and a new media room with access to the Internet and hundreds of CD-ROMS.

SECRET
CHINA

Resembling a gallery more than a store, the grand shop of fine china and crystal purveyor **William Ashley** (Manulife Centre, 55 Bloor

West, 416-964-2900) is fun to visit, even if you're just looking. Eye-catching windows overlooking Bloor are filled with colorful, luminous glassware, while the small museum-style boxes visible from the mall interior offer more intimate displays. Bargain hunters may want to wait for the annual November warehouse sale (62 Railside, south of Lawrence, two blocks east of the Don Valley Parkway), when prices on Royal Doulton, Wedgwood, and other famous-name china, crystal, and silver products drop by as much as 90 percent.

When you walk into **Hockridge China** (638 Yonge, 416-923-1668), it's like taking a step back in time. There just aren't any other china shops like this in Toronto anymore. If you're serious about collecting good china, put on your pilgrim shoes and make your way to this Mecca for lovers of Moorcroft, Royal Winton, and other esteemed offerings.

S E C R E T
CHINESE

The intersection of Dundas and Spadina marks the heart of Toronto's well-known Chinatown, where bustling food markets displaying shrimp and vegetables share the street with wicker and clothing import shops and dozens of Chinese and Vietnamese restaurants. Just north of the intersection, on the west side, **King's Noodle House** (296 Spadina Avenue, 416-598-1817) serves up a very large bowl of noodles in broth — big enough for two people, really — with slices of barbecued pork for about $5. (It's not on the menu, but for an extra $1.50 you can get a helping of Chinese greens thrown into the soup.) Directly across Spadina, the brightly lit and efficient **Swatow** (309 Spadina Avenue, 416-977-0601) makes its own noodles in the basement and delivers them to your table in heaping, inexpensive platefuls. The cuisine is Cantonese, and among Swatow's other charms local critics have discovered the excellent braised duck. For hot, hot Szechuan, try **Champion House** (480 Dundas West, 416-977-8282), and for hot-and-sour soup, dip in at **Kom Jug Yuen** (371 Spadina Avenue, 416-977-4079).

You may be overwhelmed by the choice at **Kim Moon Bakery** (438 Dundas West, 416-977-1933), where the kitchen turns out more than 300 different pastries. Buns stuffed with curried beef, black beans, or barbecued pork are popular snacks, while almond cookies and egg tarts satisfy dessert cravings. Tiny **Yung Sing Pastry Shop** (22 Baldwin, 416-979-2832), a longtime fixture on this lively little street a few blocks north of the Art Gallery of Ontario, sells delicious dim sum pastries and savory buns.

Walking north on Spadina from Dundas, you're bound to notice the impressive **Hsin Kuang Centre** (346 Spadina Avenue, at St. Andrews Street), a bright yellow building with green and red trim, two fierce stone lions guarding the front steps, and two more at the side. Rumored to have been a Chinese morgue at one time, the building is believed by many to be haunted, and the lions were installed on the advice of an exorcist to ward off unwanted spirits. Constructed in 1929 as the Labour Lyceum, it did have at least one famous dead occupant: anarchist Emma Goldman, who lay in state in the main hall in 1940. Upstairs you'll find the **Bright Pearl** (346 Spadina Avenue, second floor, 416-979-3988). The Cantonese menu is strong on seafood, including sizzling platters of black-bean scallop stuffed with shrimp, steamed Vancouver crab, bass plucked live from the tank and steamed with sesame oil, soy, and green onions, braised lobster, and invigorating hot-and-sour seafood soup. Between 11 a.m. and 4 p.m. every day, dim sum is served at Bright Pearl, but note that the price per little dish goes up during rush hour.

Nearby, but just outside the unofficial borders of Chinatown, **Jing Peking** (404 College, near Bathurst, 416-929-5691) makes great moo shu pancakes (some assembly required), pot-stickers (pan-fried pork dumplings), and spicy eggplant with fried bean curd. The menu is long and varied, and the cooking at Jing Peking is consistently robust.

Toronto has a second, smaller Chinatown in the east end, at Gerrard and Broadview, with many of the same features as the downtown neighborhood, reproduced in miniature. On the upside, the choice of restaurants is far less confusing.

If extraordinary dining is the object, and you don't object to the price, try the Cantonese cuisine at **Lai Wah Heen** (108 Chestnut, 416-977-9899). The name means "luxurious meeting place," and the menu means business, with items like coffee-smoked mango fish and braised golden conpoy (scallops, that is). The exoticism extends to the naming of dishes: lustrous peacock, for example, is an elegant salad of shredded barbecued chicken and duck, jellyfish, honeyed walnuts brushed with peanut sauce, fresh melon, and darkly ringed thousand-year-old eggs. Bring your gold card.

A suite of permanent galleries at the Royal Ontario Museum, the **T.T. Tsui Galleries of Chinese Art** (100 Queen's Park, 416-586-5549), showcases more than 1,000 ancient Chinese artifacts. In a more contemporary vein, the monumental **Chinese Railroad Workers' Memorial** (Spadina Avenue, south of Front, directly west of SkyDome), by Toronto artist Eldon Garnet, was commissioned as a public art project and installed above the railway lands running east and west along the lakeshore.

SECRET

CHOCOLATE

Belgian chocolate is the prime ingredient in pastries from **Chocolatto Patisserie and Chocolaterie** (1009 Yonge, 416-922-4011), where everything is made from scratch. Preservatives, additives, and artificial flavorings are absolutely forbidden. The kitchen creates 19 exotic cakes, including Japanese sake cake and the signature Brazilian (Belgian mousse, Brazil nut and maple sugar torte, covered in chocolate and wrapped in caramelized marzipan), as well as croissants and fruit tarts. Baked in the morning, most goods are gone by noon.

No famous trade secrets are revealed during tours of **Cadbury Chocolate Canada** (277 Gladstone, 416-530-0060), but visits to the manufacturing plant are extremely popular nonetheless. Don't be surprised if the roster is booked up a year in advance.

A small stick of homemade chocolate accompanies the coffee served at **Petit Paris Cake and Coffee Shop** (2384 Bloor West, at Jane, 416-769-9881), but if you prefer it by the kilo, just step up to the take-out counter. Every rich and fattening item on the menu at this charming Viennese-style café is made on the premises.

Homemade fudge and imported English and European candy bars abound at the **Nutty Chocolatier** (2179 Queen East, 416-698-5548), where the cookie tins, long candy counter, and old-fashioned approach will reawaken anyone's childhood sweet tooth.

S E C R E T
CIGARS

Where else can you walk in looking for a corned beef on rye and walk away with a good cigar? **Yitz's Humidor** (346 Eglinton West, 416-487-4506), hiding out in the middle of Yitz's Delicatessen, harbors a fine selection of Cuban smokes amidst the smoked meat and bagels. If you go there looking for a Cohiba or Romeo Y Julieta, however, don't overlook the corned beef, which ranks among Toronto's best.

On the southwestern edge of Yorkville, tucked behind the church at Bloor and Avenue Road (kitty-corner from the Royal Ontario Museum), the **Black & Blue Smoke Bar** (150 Bloor West, 416-920-9900) offers a high-toned retreat where you can dip into some authentic caviar, wash it down with a single-malt Scotch, and then suck on a high-priced, hand-rolled Cuban. Cigar chic at its finest.

If you enjoy smoky-voiced crooning or a little jazz piano with your stogie, check out the intimate atmosphere at **Churchill's Cigar and Wine Bar** (257 Adelaide West, 416-351-8857) or the cigar bar at **The Senator** (249 Victoria, 416-364-7517). Changing exhibits of Cuban artwork set the tone at **Havana Blues Cigar Lounge and Bistro** (890 Yonge, north of Davenport, 416-923-3294), where Cuban and Dominican cigars mix well with the malts and martinis. Along with fresh fish and fine port, you'll find a cigar room in the wine cellar at **Adega** (33 Elm, north of Yonge and Dundas, 416-977-4338), a Portuguese restaurant proffering seafood risotto and pan-seared sea bass with shrimp and saffron sauce.

According to Johnny Miller, owner of **Frank Correnti Cigars** (606 King West, 416-504-4108), his family has been selling fine Cuban smokes to Torontonians for over 100 years. His little factory on King Street — where 10 or so workers, mostly women, carefully hand-roll the leaves that Miller himself imports — supplies many local dealers, but you can buy your own here too.

S E C R E T
CINEMA

The six-theater group of **Festival Cinemas** (416-690-2600) offers a mix of repertory and second-run films throughout the year. Although the mini-chain circulates many of the same films through several theaters, the programming caters to the unique tastes of each neighborhood. The Festival membership card (only a few bucks a year) is a great deal: it cuts admission almost in half and is good at any of the cinemas. Check *NOW* for listings, or pick up a copy of the *Festival Movie Guide* outside any of the theaters. The **Revue** (400 Roncesvalles, 416-531-9959) leans toward European art films. Mostly mainstream fare is screened at the **Paradise** (1006 Bloor West, 416-537-7040) — so named for the porn theater it used to be — the **Kingsway** (3030 Bloor West, 416-236-1411), and the **Fox** (2236 Queen East, 416-691-7330). The **Royal** (606 College, 416-516-4845) is an Art Moderne–style cinema originally built in 1939 for the Pylon Theatre Company. British screen star Dame Anna Neagle apparently attended the inaugural festivities and left her footprints in concrete in the cinema foyer, although they were unfortunately lost during subsequent renovations. Under the auspices of the original owner, Rae (Lewis) Smith, a Toronto Film Society patron and editor of the

Canadian Moving Picture Digest, the Pylon cinema broke new ground in Toronto by screening foreign films. In 1997, on the verge of being knocked down after years of disuse to make room for parking, the theater was rescued and restored, with cushy new seats and a 40-foot "silver" screen. **The Music Hall** (147 Danforth, east of Broadview, 416-778-8272) was a vaudeville house known as Allen's Danforth Theatre when it opened in 1919. The building became a cinema in 1929, and in 1978 it turned into a music venue, where everyone from James Brown and John Lee Hooker to Tom Waits has performed. While The Music Hall continues to stage live concerts, the 1,600-seat theater was fitted a few years ago with a new cinema screen and state-of-the-art stereo.

No longer a member of the Festival chain, the downtown **Bloor Cinema** (506 Bloor West, at Bathurst, 416-532-6677) screens an eclectic mix of Hollywood classics, sci-fi, action flicks, and late-night cult favorites. It also hosts a series of mini-festivals, including events focusing on animation, Asian movies, short films, and award-winning commercials. Hole-in-the-wall **Ghazale** (504 Bloor West, 416-537-4417), tucked under the Bloor Cinema marquee, serves delicious take-out Lebanese specialties such as falafel sandwiches and chicken shawarma — perfect for a quick bite before, during, or after an art-house film.

Alternative art videos and Super 8 films dominate the schedule organized by **Pleasure Dome** (416-656-5577), a group dedicated to presenting cutting-edge experimental film and video. They announce four or five screenings at the beginning of each season (winter, spring, summer, and fall). Expect thematic programs such as "God, Guns, and the Weather Channel," and be forewarned that the organizing collective has a deliberate policy of noncompliance with government or other censoring or prior-approval bodies. Locations can vary, but screenings are most often held at **Cinecycle** (129 Spadina Avenue, entrance a few steps down the alleyway between buildings), which masquerades by day as a bike-repair shop and transforms into a miniature makeshift film theater whenever the need arises. A favorite with the alternative crowd, Cinecycle provides a truly unique film-going experience. Check the film listings in *NOW* or *eye*.

For serious cinephiles, **Cinematheque Ontario** (416-968-FILM) always offers a stunning lineup of the best in world cinema, building each season around particular directors, countries, or themes. Many of the presentations feature newly minted prints — and what a world of difference a crisp, luminous black-and-white print can make! Screenings take place at the Art Gallery of Ontario's **Jackman Hall** (317 Dundas West, use McCaul Street entrance, 416-979-6648). The seats are sturdy but not luxurious, and there's no pop or popcorn, but for pure film pleasure Cinematheque screenings are a must. They often sell out, so get there early. In addition to Cinematheque screenings, Jackman Hall plays host to a variety of festivals and film groups and the Gallery's own noon-hour lineup of art documentaries.

The **Ontario Place Cinesphere** (955 Lakeshore Boulevard West, 416-314-9900) is the place to experience eye-popping, head-spinning IMAX films or wide-screen classics like *Lawrence of Arabia* — all that sand!

S E C R E T
CIRCUS
❧

If you've ever dreamt of running away to live your life under the big top, you'll need some practice first. Luckily, the **Toronto School of**

Circus Arts (425 Wellington West, 416-935-0037) offers a crash course in the basics — including tight-wire walking, trampoline, hand-balancing, acrobatics, aerial skills, juggling, and the fine art of the flying trapeze. The training facilities are set up in a 15,000-square-foot space with 40-foot ceilings, formerly the press hall in the *Globe and Mail* building (444 Front Street West). If you'd rather stay in the stands, you can hire the resident **Cirque Sublime** for public or private performances.

S E C R E T

CLASSICAL

Toronto offers an extraordinarily active classical music scene, with numerous performances to choose from every day of the year. Complete listings are available in *WholeNote* (see "Other Resources").

In addition to ticketed performances by faculty and visiting musicians, free concerts are presented several times a week by students and staff at the **University of Toronto Faculty of Music** (Walter Hall or MacMillan Theatre, Edward Johnson Building, 80 Queen's Park, 416-978-3744). These include master classes with distinguished visiting conductors, evening events, and concerts and lectures in the Thursday Noon Series (12:10 p.m. in Walter Hall). The music isn't always classical — you might also catch some contemporary and historical compositions, jazz, world music, and student works.

University Settlement Music and Arts School (23 Grange, 416-598-3444) has been guiding young creative minds since 1921, with voice and instrumental classes in styles from classical to popular. The instructional program also includes drama, ballet, drawing, Chinese instruments and singing, chamber music, and choir. Student recitals take place once or twice a month, between October and June, usually at St. George the Martyr Church (205 John). Call the school for details. The school also organizes a series of professional concerts for visiting artists.

For the home listener and student of music, the **Canadian Music Centre Boutique** (Chalmers House, 20 St. Joseph, near Yonge and Wellesley, 416-961-6601) stocks more than 300 CD titles, ranging from solo instrumental works and chamber music to choral and electro-acoustic works — all written by Canadian composers and recorded by Canadian musicians. The boutique also carries published scores, manuscript paper, and educational kits on Canadian music. The century-old Chalmers House serves as national headquarters for the Canadian Music Centre (CMC), a not-for-profit organization that also maintains an extensive library of almost 13,000 published and unpublished scores by more than 500 Canadian composers, clipping files, dissertations, photos, and recordings (well-equipped listening rooms are available). The CMC is open weekdays from 9 a.m. to 5 p.m.

S E C R E T
CLIMBING

Get a grip at the **Toronto Climbing Academy** (100-A Broadview, south of Queen, 416-406-5900), an indoor rock-climbing school where you can learn how to scale cliffs and explore caves. Owned by Sasha Akalski, former coach of the Bulgarian sports climbing team, the academy is a cavernous, state-of-the-art facility featuring prefab walls molded with natural features: bulges, cracks, overhangs, and stalactites. Step-by-step climbing lessons for beginners (age 13 and up) include a day pass, harness, and climbing shoes (call for times and prices). Classes for kids 6 to 12 are available with advance notice, and clinics for experienced climbers can also be arranged.

SECRET
CNE
✦

Most people come for the fast-paced thrill of the midway — the Ferris wheels and whirligigs, candy floss and coin toss — but the Canadian National Exhibition has a history that's often overlooked. Crowds have converged on the CNE grounds since 1878, and the **Canadian National Exhibition Archives** (Exhibition Place, General Services Building, northwest corner of Fleet and Strachan, just north of the Prince's Gates, 416-263-3658) preserve the passing moment in a collection of photos, programs, film and video recordings, and artifacts. A public display is set up during the Ex, but the office is also open in the off season, when visitors can view the archives at leisure.

SECRET
COFFEE BEANS

Close to the heart of Kensington Market, the granola-esque **Moon-bean Café** (30 St. Andrews Street, 416-595-0327) sells a small but worldly selection of coffees, including the unusual Cameroon Peabody and various Latin American beans. Especially popular are the Moonbean house blends, with tempting names like Devil's Brew and Morning Buzz. The owner fires up the roasting machine at the front of the shop three times a week, including Saturday. While you're waiting for a fresh batch, pull up a painted chair and try the Hercu-latte: a triple shot of espresso served in a giant mug. Moonbean also offers a few all-day breakfast specials, including peanut butter and jam on a bagel.

Mixed Delights (2180 Queen East, at Maclean, 416-690-7649) sells about 85 brands of gourmet coffee by the pound, as well as by the cup, if you're thirsty, and a selection of teas. Watch for the mannequin in a bathing suit perched above the store sign.

All the beans at **Alternative Grounds Coffee House and Roastery** (333 Roncesvalles, 416-534-6335) are purchased from farmer-owned cooperatives and roasted onsite. The café is a relaxed, kid-friendly hangout, eclectically furnished and best in the late afternoon when the sun beams in through the large front window.

S E C R E T
CONTRACEPTION

What did people use before latex and the pill? The early Egyptians tried crocodile dung, among other things. The fascinating story of birth control methods across various cultures, from 1850 BC to the present, is explored at the **History of Contraception Museum** (Janssen-Ortho Inc., 19 Green Belt, east of Don Mills Road, between Eglinton and Lawrence, 416-449-9444). Company past-president Percy Skuy began collecting contraceptive devices, both ancient and modern, in the mid-1960s. The astonishing accumulation of condoms, sponges, candy wrappers, beaver testicles, and numerous intrauterine contraptions from around the world now fills over a dozen display cases, set up in the hallway at Janssen-Ortho. The roundup is remarkable, especially considering that most people are unlikely to save such objects. Although the artifacts are occasionally shipped to major medical meetings and are therefore temporarily unavailable for viewing, visitors can usually drop in to the museum during regular weekday business hours. But call ahead, just to be safe.

S E C R E T
CRUISING

Toronto's oldest gay bath, in operation since 1974, is **The Barracks** (56 Widmer, 416-593-0499), frequented mostly by the leather set. Facilities in this 100-year-old house — located between Richmond and Adelaide, just east of Spadina — include a "hot" dry sauna, a very dark steam room, specialty areas known as the Officers Quarters, and a snack bar lounge (where the couches, predictably, are leather). The Barracks Toy Store sells hundreds of playtime trinkets, from lubes, pumps, and plugs (no, these ain't for the car) to tit clamps and wrist restraints. Open 24 hours a day.

Conveniently located smack in the middle of the Gay Village, **The Spa on Maitland** (66 Maitland, 416-925-1571), above the Superfresh Mart, sprawls over the entire second floor of the building, at the corner of Church, one block south of Wellesley. The Spa seems to have two of everything — two saunas, two steam rooms, two showers, even two screening rooms, one for feature films and one for adult flicks. It's also the only steam bath in town with a liquor license.

The very dark and definitely subterranean **Cellar** (78 Wellesley East, 416-975-1799) secludes itself behind an unmarked black door, easy to walk past without noticing. Downstairs, once you've paid at the cage for a room and entered the underground lair, cruising begins in earnest.

SECRET
CUBAN

Don't let the old sign for Julie's Snack Bar fool you, with its weathered Coca-Cola ads and promise of take-out service. The new owners of **Julie's Restaurant and Bar** (202 Dovercourt, south of Dundas, 416-532-7397) have transmogrified the dowdy neighborhood shop into a steamy Latin cantina, complete with authentic Cuban cuisine and refreshing mojitos (my favorite drink, concocted of white rum and soda over crushed ice, laced with lime juice, and sweetened with sugar and fresh mint leaves). For 30 years, beginning in the mid-1960s, restaurateur Julie Berezansky catered to the local blue-collar crowd. But since reopening the restaurant in 1995, her daughter Sylvia and partner Jesús have been serving affordable tapas, including a tart grouper ceviche, oily shrimp in garlic and white wine, corn fritters, and deep-fried plantain stuffed with avocado.

SECRET
CYBERCULTURE

Toronto cybercafés have come and gone over the years, each one in search of a business model that successfully combines coffee and computers. Happily, several among the current crop have realized that good food is an important ingredient, and the accent has shifted from cyber to café. True to its name, **Insomnia Internet Bar/Café** (563 Bloor West, at the Bathurst subway, 416-588-3907) stays open into the wee hours (3 a.m. weeknights, 5 a.m. Friday and Saturday). A few couches are tucked away at the back for those in search of a living-room ambience, and several curtain-walled cubicles are available for those who don't like to surf in public. Service is perky, and the fare is quite tasty.

Free access to the Net is available at most branches of the Toronto Public Library, including the **Metropolitan Toronto Reference Library** (789 Yonge, one block north of Bloor, 416-393-7141), where you'll also find the Digital Design Studio. For a fee, you can use high-quality computers, scanners, printers, and design software. But remember, this isn't a café, so there's no coffee allowed.

SECRET
DANCE

Dedicated to preserving the works of Canadian choreographers, the **Dance Collection Danse** (145 George, near Queen and Jarvis, 416-365-3233) is a fascinating archival repository of photographs, films, costumes (including what is believed to be the oldest Canadian theatrical dance costume, made in Ottawa in 1918 for Nesta Williams, as well as Maud Allan's *Salome* costume made circa 1906 in Berlin), scrapbooks, dance programs, props, and other related artifacts. Built primarily from personal collections and regular visits to the flea market at St. Lawrence Market, the archive largely represents dance activity in Canada before 1950. Doubling as a small publishing house, Dance Collection Danse produces works like *Toronto Dance Teachers, 1825–1925*, which are available onsite, by mail order, or at Theatrebooks (see "Secret Theater"). The collection is open by appointment only.

Toronto offers dance lovers a healthy variety of stage stomping. The **National Ballet of Canada** (416-345-9686, www.national.ballet.ca) performs regularly at the **Hummingbird Centre for the Performing Arts** (1 Front East, 416-393-7469), while the **Premiere Dance Theatre** (207 Queen's Quay West, 416-973-4000) is home to an excellent series of Canadian and international contemporary dance performances. These programs are well known and well attended. Less attention, however, is given to Toronto's independent dance

community, which offers challenging and often much cheaper entertainment. Makeshift "stages" have been known to appear in empty doughnut stores and unused warehouses. Several small theaters and rehearsal halls, including **Dancemakers** (927 Dupont, 416-535-8880) and **Winchester Street Theatre** (80 Winchester), also feature dance events. To find out what's on stage — or off stage, in some cases — look for the dance listings in *NOW* (see "Other Resources") or drop by **Dance Umbrella of Ontario** (490 Adelaide West, between Portland and Maud, 416-504-6429) and check the flyers on the bulletin board.

Dance Ontario (130 Spadina Avenue, Suite 203-A, 416-204-1082) organizes **DanceWeekend** every January to showcase Toronto's professional dance companies and independent artists. Two days of dance — in styles stretching from ballet and modern to flamenco, kathak, African, Caribbean, jazz, and hip hop — take place at various Harbourfront locations, including the south atrium in Queen's Quay Terminal. Dance Ontario also organizes **Danceworks**, Toronto's longest running contemporary dance series.

Gaining momentum with every annual recurrence, the mid-August **Fringe Festival of Independent Dance Artists** (416-410-4291) invigorates the Toronto dance card with cutting-edge contemporary performances at half a dozen indoor and outdoor locations. Dancers and choreographers from as far away as Japan, Sweden, the US, Quebec, and elsewhere in Canada join innovative local performers in a series of short programs.

Another annual event well worth attending is **Moving Pictures: The Festival of Dance on Film and Video** (416-961-5424). Screenings take place in early October at such venues as the Art Gallery of Ontario and the Rivoli, while visiting filmmakers might lead workshops on such topics as guerrilla video tactics.

Pegasus Children's Dance Centre (361 Glebeholme, at Coxwell and Danforth, 416-469-2799, www.pegasusdance.com) provides an atmosphere in which children can explore and express their creative spirit, physically, visually, and musically. Classes in creative movement, ballet, jazz, tap, and modern dance are taught by some of Toronto's top dance and art educators, under the watchful eye of director Jane Davis-Munro. While their children are taking part in a class at Pegasus, parents can get physical in the nearby **Physical Harmony Pilates Studio** (361 Glebeholme, 416-406-4599), where certified instructors lead Pilates classes.

SECRET

DEAD HOUSE

Winters are cold in Toronto, and the ground freezes up pretty solidly. Pity the poor gravedigger in the mid-1800s, when a pick and shovel were the only available tools of the trade and carving a six-foot pit out of the cold earth could take forever. Oh, hell, why not wait until spring, when the ground is more forgiving? Well, that's exactly what the Catholic clergy decided in 1855 when they built the **St. Michael's Dead House** (St. Michael's Cemetery, 1414 Yonge, south of St. Clair). Designed by Toronto architect Joseph Sheard — who also designed numerous schools, churches, and private homes around town and later served as the city's mayor (1871–72) — this elegant, octagonal stone building was used as a winter vault to store bodies until the spring thaw. St. Michael's Cemetery was established during a particularly tragic period, when the potato famine and subsequent typhus epidemic drove boatloads of Irish emigrants to Canada in the late

1840s. Quarantine sheds were built along King Street to house the sick and dying. The city's first Catholic cemetery, St. Paul's, located near Queen and Parliament, was rapidly filling to capacity. So St. Michael's was created farther north in the suburb of Deer Park, well beyond the city limits at that time. Most of the original iron, zinc, and limestone memorials in St. Michael's have been replaced by granite markers, although a few iron ones remain. More than 29,000 people are now buried in the 10-acre site, including John Pickford Hennessey, grandfather of screen legend Mary Pickford (born Gladys Smith in Toronto). In the 1920s, the strip of land fronting on Yonge Street was sold for commercial development, so the cemetery is now hidden from view, like some private courtyard, accessible only through a narrow gateway. St. Michael's Dead House is no longer used — but if you're visiting on a cold winter's day, you should peek in through one of the small windows, just to be certain.

SECRET
DENTISTRY

If dental drills and root canals are the last things you associate with a leisure-time activity, a visit to the **Dentistry Museum** (Faculty of Dentistry, University of Toronto, 124 Edward, 416-979-4900) may change your mind. Comfortable chairs and discomforting tools (including a few of the homemade variety) and a collection of historical and innovative toothbrushes — as well as paintings, prints, and numerous other objects — document the fascinating history of dentistry. And the Waterloo dentures, made from military molars (and other teeth) extracted from corpses after the Battle of Waterloo, will leave a lasting impression. Admission is free, but zero staff and limited funds mean the museum cannot keep regular hours. If you have a pressing need, you may be able to book a private appointment. Otherwise, watch for the annual Saturday open house early in October.

Another appointment-only adventure awaits you at **The Wedge Gallery** (676 Richmond West, Suite 206, 416-504-9641), a small exhibition area about the size of a hallway — well, actually, it is a hallway — in the home of Toronto's coolest dentist, Dr. Kenneth Montague. His airy, ultramodern loft in a former knitting factory, designed by graphic artist Del Terrelonge, integrates a public space within a private residence, heightening the intimacy of the viewer's encounter with art. Since 1997, Montague has been showing mostly photographic work by black artists, including Michael Chambers and James VanDerZee. Call ahead to book a visit, but don't try to book any dental work at the same time, because Dr. Montague does his drilling elsewhere. In contrast to the cool aesthetic of his Richmond Street digs, his dental office near Bloor and Bathurst exudes a relaxing Caribbean vibe. The potted palm tree, art prints, pictures of Jamaica, and hip hop or reggae tunes emanating from the sound system create a decidedly nonclinical environment, one that provides a type of art and music therapy for his patients. One can only wish that more dentists were so creatively disposed.

SECRET
DESIGN

Crammed floor to ceiling with books on architecture, antiques and collectibles, design, and graphic arts, **Another Man's Poison**

(29 McCaul, 416-593-6451) is a treasure trove of Canadian, international, and out-of-print titles. Another outlet for the printed word on advertising and design is **Swipe Books** (477 Richmond West, 416-363-1332), where you'll find books on art direction, copywriting, branding, information graphics, and design theory. You can also pick up some fancy fonts for your computer and a few designer items from Alessi and others.

Product exhibits, manufacturers' catalogues, and samples are available for viewing in the resource center at **Designer's Walk** (168 Bedford, second floor, 416-961-1211). Built as a central hub for the design community, this five-building complex houses more than 30 showrooms for international collections and hosts design-related seminars and events. This is the spot to browse for everything from antiques and appliances to fabrics, flooring, and furniture.

S E C R E T
DINERS
❧

Located across the road from a wrecker's yard, the **Canary Grill** (409 Front East, 416-364-9943) is a real landmark, popping up regularly in Canadian films and TV. Built in the late 1850s to house a public school and later converted to a small hotel known as the Eastern Star, the ramshackle building now houses a few small businesses. Breakfast and burgers at the Canary may not make you sing, but the meatloaf's pretty good.

Grandfather, father, and son work side by side at the aptly named **Patrician Grill** (219 King East, 416-364-4841), which attracts student diners from nearby George Brown College, including aspiring chefs from the hospitality program. But nobody comes here looking for health-conscious cooking or an innovative fusion of Eastern and Western cuisine — they come for the hot turkey sandwich.

SECRET
DISCIPLINE

Feeling stressed? Ever wish you could just crawl back into your childhood crib and cry like a baby? Well, the adult baby nursery at **Madame de Sade's Bondage Hotel** (159 Gerrard East, 416-413-0827) may be just the thing. Or perhaps you'd prefer the boarding school of discipline, "For Gentlemen in need of correction through Corporal Punishment and/or Forced Feminization," an academy that harkens back to old English boarding school traditions. Additional scenarios in Madame de Sade's repertoire include sensory deprivation, rope bondage, prison play, and various other psychodramas. But remember, no sex please, we're Canadian — the bondage and role-playing at Madame de Sade's are strictly a form of adult theater. This novel bed-and-breakfast establishment is run by the buxom Terri-Jean Bedford, Toronto's most infamous dominatrix. Formerly known as the Millicent Farnsworth Sissy Maid Academy and Charm School, the business has been expanded to accommodate overnight guests. Continental or pancake breakfast is included — just the thing to get your strength up after a night in the medieval dungeon. Private suites are available, with special weekend rates for honeymoon couples. Reservations required. Madame de Sade also offers psychic readings, a tea room, and a vintage fetish boutique, featuring Victorian and gothic apparel, 1950s prom dresses, girdles and corsets, garter belts, and, of course, fetish footwear.

S E C R E T
DOWN EAST

Among the many communities that bless Toronto's cultural landscape, we too rarely encounter the down-home hospitality of Canadians from our own East Coast. Fortunately, Conrad Beaubien and Cynthia Riordon at the **Down East Gift Shop and Gallery** (508 Bathurst, at College, 416-925-1642) are more than willing to engage in friendly conversation with folks who drop by. Riordon is a native New Brunswicker, hailing from Bathurst, while Beaubien — an independent filmmaker and creator of the long-running *Sketches of Our Town* documentary series — was born in Ottawa but has spent enough time down east to become an "adopted Miramichier." Here, at their well-stocked Toronto outpost, they sell Maritime newspapers and just enough hardtack and coal candy to inspire a nostalgic reaction — even if you come from away. But mostly, they specialize in folk art and other "awful good stuff" from Atlantic Canada, including hand-knit socks, pottery, partridgeberry relish, jewelry, and oilskin caps of both traditional and contemporary design. A corner of the shop is devoted to Maud Lewis reproductions and other souvenir objects bearing images from the folk-art oeuvre of the self-taught painter from Nova Scotia.

S E C R E T
DRUGS

A thematic history of drug use and abuse is presented by the **Centre for Addiction and Mental Health** (33 Russell, one block north of College, east of Spadina, 416-535-8501) in a permanent hall display, highlighted by opium pipes and water bongs. These objects and photos represent only a small portion of the artifacts, publications, and audiovisuals in the center's extensive collection. You can borrow library materials and screen videos in the viewing room. Admission is free. Aside from its role as a research facility, the center is also a public hospital providing direct patient care for people with mental health and addiction problems, an education and training institute, and a community-based organization providing health promotion and prevention services across Ontario.

S E C R E T
ELEVATORS

Getting to the **Elevator Gallery** (9 Davies, fifth floor, 416-406-3131) is half the fun, especially if you like riding old warehouse elevators. The warehouse itself is located near Queen Street East and Broadview Avenue, overlooking the Don Valley Parkway. The gallery is dedicated to raising (insert elevator pun here) the profile of established and emerging contemporary photographers. Unlike traditional galleries, Elevator doesn't attempt to act as a long-term dealer for photographers. Rather, it makes the space available as a rental and lets the artists keep any exhibition sales proceeds. The rest of the business is devoted to archival framing, in a shop just behind the gallery.

Toronto's first electric elevator still operates, in all of its swanky oak-panel and brass-button glory, in the wedge-shaped **Gooderham Building** (49 Wellington). Built in 1892, 10 years before its New York cousin, Toronto's flatiron building derives its shape from the triangular intersection of Wellington, laid out according to the city's grid design, and Front Street, which follows the Lake Ontario shoreline. The elevator's maximum capacity is five people, including the operator, and even with a lighter load it takes 27 seconds to climb five stories. Nevertheless, it was a luxury in its heyday, when distillery owner and financial kingpin George Gooderham installed the conveyance to carry him to his top-floor office. The elevator shaft was originally an open space running up the middle of the winding staircase, but fire regulations have since required a drywall enclosure, robbing riders of the complete old-world effect. Still, stepping into the elevator itself is enough to push your nostalgia buttons.

If you're a vertical transportation fanatic, you'll already know about the six high-speed glass capsules that race up the CN **Tower** (301 Front, 416-868-6937) at 24 kilometers (15 miles) per hour. The elevator operators will happily answer any of your questions on the way up, but you have to ask fast, because the entire ride takes only 58 seconds — it's much shorter than the wait in the ticket lineup to get on. These elevators don't actually go all the way to the top, however. The first leg stops at the lookout level, and one floor down you'll find the famous glass floor (go ahead, jump up and down on it!) and outdoor observation deck. For the last 33 floors, you have to switch elevators (separate ticket required) and ride up to the Sky Pod, where there's an unobstructed 360-degree view — and the unmistakable feeling of swaying in the wind.

SECRET
ESPIONAGE

The shabby decor at **Spytech** (2028 Yonge, 416-482-8588) gives the impression of a fly-by-night operation, but Ursula Lebana's company has been selling high-tech surveillance and security gizmos for years. In fact, "spy-by-night" might be a more accurate description. Pinhole video cameras, microphones concealed in ordinary lipstick tubes, night-vision goggles, miniature KGB-style binoculars (suitable for the opera), letter-bomb detectors, and countersurveillance equipment are available to the public — for less money than you might expect. Budget-conscious fledgling spies can certainly afford the sunglasses with built-in rearview mirrors, and anyone with small valuables to protect but no vault to lock them in will appreciate the safe cans: look-alike product containers (like Lemon Pledge canisters or Campbell's soup tins) designed to hold cash and jewelry. Lebana and her staff are happy to demonstrate their many products, and shopping at Spytech is certain to give you a new (and discreet) perspective on the world.

SECRET
ETHIOPIAN

The staple element of Ethiopian cuisine is injera, a spongy, slightly sour-tasting flatbread used as an edible plate. Made from a fermented millet grain called tef, injera is high in iron and essentially free of gluten, the protein that often causes an allergic reaction to wheat.

Cooked on one side only, in a large, flat clay pan, it is consumed by tearing off small bits and using them to scoop up various stews. Meals are eaten communally, with everyone ripping and tearing from the same bread — in Ethiopia, it's believed that people who eat from the same plate will never betray one another.

Several Ethiopian and Eritrean restaurants are scattered along Bloor Street, west of Christie Pits, although none has been established long enough to gain the following enjoyed by **Queen of Sheba** (1051 Bloor West, west of Dufferin, 416-536-4162), the reigning purveyor of Ethiopian cuisine. Groups of diners can share large mixed platters of meat stew and vegetables heaped in little mounds on injera.

Behind the unlikely façade of a faux Austrian ski chalet, complete with wooden-log exterior, you'll find **Chef Wondiy** (1671 Bloor West, east of Keele, 416-530-1609) serving traditional Ethiopian fare. When this restaurant first opened on the outskirts of a historically Polish neighborhood, the African/European schizophrenic split was reflected in the restaurant's menu, where exotic dishes like doro wat (spicy chicken stew with eggs) and kitfo (a variation on steak tartare) were offered side by side with pizza and crepes. The owner was clearly hedging his bets. Happily, his clientele expressed a clear preference for Ethiopian fare, and the other stuff has since been dropped — that is, the kitchen doesn't cook it anymore, while the employees instruct you to ignore that half of the menu, which has yet to be reprinted. So, concentrate instead on the various vegetarian and meat stews, heavy with green chilies and served with rolls of injera. There's even a short breakfast menu, featuring cold shiro or flax with injera crumbs and a morning salad of seedless tomato, raw onion, and green chilies.

Not far from the intersection of Yonge and Bloor, **Ethiopian House** (4 Irwin, 416-923-5438) offers both beef and vegetarian dishes, served gracefully in a quiet atmosphere. Follow your meal with an Ethiopian coffee, prepared at your table in a traditional ceremony and presented with an aromatic burning of cardamom and frankincense.

S E C R E T
FASHIONS

During the 1920s Prohibition era, a man from Buffalo smuggled a beaded flapper dress into this country by wearing it under his own clothes when he crossed the border. Many years later, his wife donated that dress, and told the story of its arrival in Canada, to the **Fashion Resource Centre** (Seneca College of Applied Arts and Technology, 1750 Finch East, 416-491-5050, ext. 2578). Similarly colorful stories accompany many other pieces of apparel in the collection, now comprising more than 8,000 items made or worn in Canada. Begun in 1988, the center is a teaching resource for Seneca students — a working library of primarily Euro-Canadian fashions dating from as early as 1840. Members of the public are welcome to visit (by appointment, and for a fee) for a close-up inspection of how garments from an earlier era were made. Yves St. Laurent gowns from the early 1950s might catch your eye or perhaps the beautifully structured rayon day-dress from the '40s with the lively piano print. If you're partial to a particular type of clothing, alert the volunteer staff ahead of time, and they will happily tailor your tour of the "big closet" to meet your interests.

S E C R E T
FAST FOOD

Waiter on Wheels (416-751-9684) brings dinner from more than 60 Toronto restaurants directly to your doorstep, and the sister company **Dial-a-Bottle** (416-751-4222) quickly delivers anything in stock at the LCBO. The bill for a bottle is $6 plus the price of the plonk. The company's repertoire also includes bagged groceries and prescription drugs.

Restaurants on the Go (416-932-3999, www.foodroute.com) has been delivering meals from fine Toronto restaurants since 1995. The delivery area is divided into 11 sections, from Lake Ontario north to Finch, bounded by Dufferin in the west and Victoria Park in the east. Your restaurant choices are determined by your location, and delivery time is usually about an hour — not particularly fast, but the food is freshly made. Pick up a menu guide, or log on to the Web site to browse the available cuisines.

S E C R E T
FIRE HALLS

When the Toronto Fire Department made the leap from volunteer force to full-time department in the mid-1870s, three new stations were built, including **No. 8 Hose Station** (132 Bellevue, at College, west of Spadina, 416-923-9466). The lovely yellow- and red-brick building was completed in 1878, and in 1899 the lookout tower was extended to its current height of 110 feet. Nighttime strollers along College Street have been known to mistake the tower's illuminated clock face for a full moon rising against a dark sky. In 1911, the horse-drawn fire wagon at No. 8 was replaced by the city's first motorized fire engine. Today, a 1924 Bickell pumper still sits inside the station (new truck bays for modern equipment have been added on the south side), and historic photographs and other fire department memorabilia line the walls. If the firefighters aren't elsewhere attending to a blaze, one might be happy to show you around the old station. Ironically, the No. 8 Hose Station itself broke out in flames in 1972 — while vacant for restoration, the building was torched by an arsonist and suffered serious damage — but it has been fully restored to its original state.

Several other historic fire halls grace Toronto neighborhoods. In Yorkville, **Fire Hall No. 10** (34 Yorkville) has been in action since 1876. The tower here, as elsewhere, was used primarily for hanging up fire hoses to drain dry. A plaque bearing five symbols — anvil, beer barrel, brick mold, bull's head, and jack plane — is mounted on the tower, but it has little to do with firefighting. It is the Yorkville coat of arms (the images represent the occupations of the first town councilors), and it originally adorned the town hall . . . until a fire destroyed the building.

Completed in 1906, **Kew Beach Fire Hall No. 17** (1904 Queen East, east of Woodbine) was designed in the Queen Anne Revival style, while the stepped gable on the street façade borrows from Flemish Renaissance commercial buildings.

Poking up from behind a modern storefront on Toronto's most famous downtown street, the picturesque Victorian tower built in 1870–72 is all that remains of **Fire Hall No. 3** (488 Yonge, between Grosvenor and Grenville, a block and a half north of College).

Conversely, the trademark tower is the part missing from **Fire Hall No. 4**, built in 1859 but converted to a playhouse in 1971. The **Alumnae Theatre** (70 Berkeley, 416-364-4170) is now the permanent home of the University Alumnae Dramatic Club, founded in 1918 by women graduates of University College and the oldest active theater company in Canada.

Another vintage fire truck, a 1936 Bickell, forms part of the display at the **North York Fire Department Museum** (Station 19, 59 Curlew, at Lawrence, 416-338-9188). Photographs and objects illustrate the evolution of firefighting equipment, beginning in the 1930s, with a focus on North York's history. Free tours are offered, and kids can put on miniature versions of the uniform and rubber boots for a souvenir photo or buy imitation helmets to take home.

Open houses, demonstrations, and other public events are scheduled during **Fire Prevention Week**, around mid-October. At all other times, free tours of any fire station in town can be arranged by phoning 416-338-9050. That's also the number to call if you'd like to arrange a private tour of the fireboat *William Lyon Mackenzie* (Station 35, 11 Queen's Quay West) or to find out about the fire department's annual **Kidsummer** events: a day in July and a day in August when children can participate in educational firefighting games and watch a fire suppression show and rescue simulations.

SECRET

FIRST NATIONS

The **Native Canadian Centre of Toronto** (16 Spadina Road, north of Bloor, 416-964-9087) holds drumming and dancing socials every Thursday from 6 p.m. to 8 p.m. Every other Thursday, the evening extends to 10 p.m. with a potluck dinner. Cree language classes and traditional teaching circles on Tuesday complement the busy schedule of painting classes, martial arts, and other programs. The center is particularly popular with seniors and kids, and anyone interested in touring the building and hearing about what goes on there is welcome to drop by. Downstairs, the cafeteria is open on weekdays for lunch. In mid-April, the Native Canadian Centre also organizes an annual three-day Native elders conference, held at a downtown hotel.

Admirers of soapstone and whalebone can visit the TD **Bank Gallery of Inuit Art** (79 Wellington, Maritime Life Tower, main floor, 416-982-8473), designed to showcase the bank's corporate collection of approximately 200 sculptures and a selection of early prints. Guided tours of the display can be arranged with advance notice.

The **Joseph Brant Museum** (1240 North Shore, Burlington, 905-634-3556), built on a tract of land granted by King George III in 1800 to the Six Nations war chief, displays artifacts once belonging to Brant, as well as items found in the area. Following his years as an interpreter for the British Indian Department and his later military exploits during the American Revolution on behalf of the British, Brant retired to Burlington Bay to translate passages of the Bible into Mohawk. The museum is a 1938 reconstruction of the original house and contains a furnished parlor, a Woodland Indian gallery celebrating Brant's Mohawk ancestry, and an exhibit exploring Burlington's past.

SECRET

FISH AND CHIPS

Unless you're traveling with a football team, don't order any extra fries at **Harbord Fish and Chips** (147 Harbord, 416-925-2225) — a single order will easily feed two or three people. It's a mystery where all the potatoes are stored, because the white brick building is rather small, with no indoor seating or eating, just a stand-up take-out counter. Outside, a couple of picnic tables are parked right at road-side, so you can eat there if you're not driving away with your order.

Pacific halibut and PEI potatoes are faithful partners on the menu at **Penrose Fish and Chips** (600 Mount Pleasant, 416-483-6800). The cooler is stocked with bottles of Seamans' Old Fashioned Pop from down east, and on Friday there's homemade lemon meringue pie. In business for more than 50 years, and located amid Mount Pleasant's antique alley (see "Secret Antiques"), Penrose maintains the look and feel of an earlier era: red leatherette booths, aqua paint, stuffed swordfish adorning the wall, and nostalgic black-and-white photos of a younger Toronto.

While Penrose sticks to halibut, the folks at **Len Duckworth's Fish and Chips** (2638 Danforth, east of Main, 416-699-5865) know there's plenty of fish in the sea. Their unusually broad selection goes beyond the reliable halibut to include hake, haddock, sole, and the somewhat pricier orange roughy. This classic diner with comfortable booths has been slinging fish and chips since 1930. A scoop of scallops accompanies the halibut combo at **Kingsway Fish and Chips** (3062 Bloor West, 416-233-3355), where the dessert menu proffers Chudleigh's pies.

SECRET

FRENCH

Kensington Market hasn't been a serious dinner destination for ages, so the recent arrival of **La Palette** (256 Augusta, 416-929-4900) is a refreshing reversal of fortune. Good steak frites, delicious sea bass, Basque salad with port-glazed chicken livers, a vigorous wine list, and an absence of snooty service make this casual bistro a neighborhood favorite. The room is small and fills up quickly, so go early or make reservations. Beer drinkers take note: La Palette also stocks almost every French and Québécois beer available in Ontario, including the dark amber La Choulette.

Service at **Le Paradis Brasserie-Bistro** (166 Bedford, north of Davenport, 416-921-0995) is inconsistent — sometimes it borders on Parisian indifference, at other times it's perfectly pleasant — but the cooking, at least, is reliable. This is the place for healthy portions of solid French fare at great prices.

SECRET

FRISBEE GOLF

Courtesy of the Orange Crush Bottling Company, which donated funds in 1980, Toronto has a permanent Frisbee golf course on **Ward's Island**. A series of 18 pole-holes — metal baskets set on poles, surmounted by hanging chains designed to stop the Frisbee in flight — is set up near the picnic area, among the trees and bushes that provide natural obstacles. Serious players prefer specialized, heavier-than-normal discs, but any Frisbee will do. To get there, take the Ward's Island ferry from the docks at the foot of Bay Street (call 416-392-8193 for schedules). When you disembark on the island, follow the path to the right.

S E C R E T

GARBAGE

Where does it all go? If you've ever wondered what happens to your garbage after it leaves the curb, or been curious about recycling, the **City of Toronto Works and Emergency Services** department (416-392-9652) offers enlightenment through public tours at various facilities. Transfer stations mark the first stage, where you can watch the process of dumping, compaction, and reloading into transport trailers for shipment to landfill sites or processing plants. Both the **Disco Road Transfer Station** (120 Disco, Etobicoke) and the **Scarborough Transfer Station** (Transfer Place, Markham Road at Nugget, Scarborough) provide one-hour weekday tours by appointment. Tours can also be arranged at the **Materials Recovery Facility** (400 Commissioners), where reusable plastic, steel, aluminum, and glass collected through the blue box program are shipped for sorting. (Newsprint, cardboard, telephone books, and magazines are processed elsewhere.) Finally, the history, construction, and daily operation of a sanitary landfill, including leaf composting and vehicle weigh scales, are fully explained on tours of the **Keele Valley Landfill Site** (in Maple, approximately a one-hour drive north of Toronto). Visitors are treated to a one-hour presentation, followed by a 30-minute tour, by appointment only (minimum five people). All tours must be booked at least two weeks in advance.

S E C R E T

GARDENS

Don't expect to hear anything musical when you visit the **Toronto Music Garden** (Queen's Quay West, midway between Bathurst and Spadina), except the ambient soundtrack of passing traffic or the wind through the tall grasses. Do expect a swirling, visual concert of flowers, rocks, and intermittent sculptural crescendos. Inspired by the first suite of J.S. Bach's *Suites for Unaccompanied Cello*, this two-acre green space unfurling along the Lake Ontario shoreline is the result of a unique collaboration between landscape designer Julie Moir Messervy and cellist Yo-Yo Ma. The six dance movements of the first suite are rendered as a landscape set to music: the curves and bends of an undulating river, punctuated by almost 500 tons of sparkling granite, excavated from a glacial moraine near the village of Moonstone, Ontario (prelude); a forest grove of wandering trails (allemande); a wildflower meadow traversed by a swirling path (courante); an arc-shaped conifer grove (sarabande); a formal flower parterre with circular steel pavilion (minuet); and jaunty, oversized grass steps resembling an amphitheater (gigue). Certainly, a bird's-eye balcony view from any of the condominiums lining the north side of Queen's Quay would afford someone a complete picture of the formal design, but the earthbound experience of walking through the garden (or skipping

or running, or even stopping to sit and meditate, as your own sense of tempo dictates) is an immensely more intimate encounter. During the summer, volunteer guides from the **Civic Garden Centre** give tours (call 416-338-0338 for times).

Thousands of tropical and subtropical plants thrive in the greenhouses and conservatory at **Allan Gardens** (south side of Carlton, between Jarvis and Sherbourne, 416-392-7288). Although the original structure, opened by the Prince of Wales in 1860, burned down at the turn of the century, it was replaced in 1909 by the beautiful, glass-domed, Victorian-style Palm House. Additional greenhouses were built in later years, for a total of six. Open year round (9 a.m. to 4 p.m. weekdays, 10 a.m. to 5 p.m. weekends), and entirely free, Allan Gardens is a particularly welcoming oasis in dark December, when the Victorian Christmas flower show is abloom. (Devotees of Scottish poet Robert Burns take note: you may pay homage to his creative genius at the life-size bronze statue by Edinburgh sculptor D.W. Stevenson, located at the east end of the 13-acre park.)

SECRET

GAY VILLAGE

Although significant numbers of gays and lesbians live elsewhere in the metropolis, the downtown intersection of Church and Wellesley marks the center of Toronto's preeminent gay neighborhood. A few strides to the south, the broad steps of the **Second Cup** (546 Church, 416-964-2457) offer a perfect place to sit and gaze at the daily parade. The **519 Community Centre** (519 Church, 416-392-6874) provides an anchor for the area with community resources and meeting rooms for gay and lesbian groups, while the green space next to the community center, **Cawthra Park**, is a favorite warm-weather spot for sunbathers. The park is also the site of North America's first permanent AIDS memorial, an elegant array of stone plinths bearing engraved metal plaques, set along a garden walkway. Drop in to the second-floor offices of *Xtra* (491 Church, 416-925-6665), Toronto's gay and lesbian biweekly, where you can pick up copies of the free paper, as well as issues from other Canadian cities, or view occasional displays from the Canadian Lesbian and Gay Archives (see "Secret Archives"). For information on upcoming events, call the paper's Gay Community Information Line (416-925-9872).

The parameters of the village are roughly marked by Bloor, Yonge, Carlton, and Jarvis, although Church Street, hopping with shops, restaurants, and bars both north and south of Wellesley, is the commercial hub. Exclusively gay and lesbian artists exhibit at **O'Connor Gallery** (97 Maitland, 416-921-7149). Two mainstay bars on the boystown strip are **Woody's** (467 Church, 416-972-0887), featuring theme nights and a well-known weekend brunch, and **The Stables** (418 Church, one block south of Carlton, 416-977-4702). **Crews Toronto** (508 Church, 416-972-1662) features live drag shows, an occasional band, a pool table, and a summertime patio.

Buddies in Bad Times Theatre (12 Alexander, 416-975-8555) continues to offer camp, comedy, and cutting-edge drama in its lively schedule of plays and performances, which includes the annual three-week Rhubarb! festival of riotous new works. The front section of Buddies doubles as a bar, where eclectic late-night performances under the banner of **Tallulah's Cabaret** unfold on Friday and Saturday. Both evenings attract a mixed crowd. Buddies is also a venue to watch for readings and special events, particularly around Easter, Halloween, and other holiday occasions.

Fine dining in a vaguely Mediterranean vein, not to mention great martinis, can be found at the chic **Byzantium** (499 Church, 416-920-3859), where the music tends toward jazz and Broadway classics. The food is also fabulous at **Spiral** (582 Church, 416-964-1102), particularly the vegetarian frittata served at brunch.

The village becomes appropriately festive during **Gay Pride Week** (416-927-7433, www.pridetoronto.com), toward the end of June. Church Street is a key stretch along the route of the Gay Pride Parade, a tumultuously popular annual event when hundreds of marching participants strut and shake their stuff to the music (sometimes with costume and sometimes without), wave community banners, and celebrate in unison as thousands of spectators crowd the sidewalks and cheer them on. The Dyke March takes to the streets the day before.

S E C R E T
GERMAN

The **Goethe Institut** (163 King West, 416-593-5257, hot line 416-593-5258) is the central hub of German cultural activity in Toronto. The public lending library emphasizes contemporary German literature and language, retains an extensive collection of German daily newspapers and magazines, and carries talking books, CDs (from classical to rock), slides, and videos. During library hours, you can even watch international German television. In addition to offering language courses, the institute sponsors an intensive program of lectures, films, dance and theater performances, art exhibitions, and music, which take place at a variety of locations.

It's a bit of a pilgrimage to get there, and it's only open on Sunday from 11 a.m. to 5 p.m., but the volunteer-run **German Canadian Heritage Museum** (6650 Hurontario, Mississauga) preserves a few worthy objects marking the German contribution to early Canadian culture and settlement. The display includes artifacts from the beginnings of the German press in Canada (newspapers, Bibles, language books, certificates), a fairy-tale corner, and miniature models of a blacksmith shop, a sawmill, and the Conestoga wagon commonly used by German-speaking immigrants coming north from Pennsylvania in the 19th century.

S E C R E T

GIRL GUIDES

Guidebooks, photographs, uniforms, and insignia are among the treasured holdings of the **Girl Guides of Canada Archives** (50 Merton, 416-487-5281). The collection, which includes objects dating back as early as 1912, is open by appointment on weekdays only. A small satellite exhibit at **Casa Loma** (1 Austin Terrace, 416-923-1171) celebrates the contributions of Lady Mary Pellatt, wife of the castle's builder, to Girl Guides in Canada.

It's cookie season every spring, from early April to mid-May, when hundreds of Girl Guides hit the street flogging boxes of treats in their annual fund-raising drive. You can get a head start on the season at the **Girl Guides of Canada Store** (downstairs at 50 Merton, 416-487-5281, ext. 227), where they get stock early, and you may even find a few boxes left over in late May. Throughout the year, the store sells a startling variety of Girl Guide gear, from uniforms and camping equipment to fridge magnets, puzzlegrams, camp crests, charm bracelets, and books by the dozen. They've even got cookie tins and porcelain plates embellished with pictures of classic Girl Guide cookies.

S E C R E T

GLENDON

When York University was founded in 1959, the first classes were actually held at **Glendon College** (2275 Bayview, at Lawrence, 416-736-2100), a small campus occupying the former estate of E.R. Wood and Agnes Euphemia Wood. Perched on the edge of the Don River Valley, the estate was built in the early 1920s on the site of a pioneer farm. The Woods's elegant manor house, Glendon Hall, is renowned for its German wrought-iron work, plaster moldings, and sweeping half-oval walnut staircase, illuminated by a skylight. The **Glendon Art Gallery** (416-487-6721), a later addition to the house, presents monthly exhibits of contemporary art. Downstairs, replacing a former ballroom, you'll find the **Café de la Terrasse** (416-487-6703), with a lovely back patio overlooking the valley. The estate is beautifully landscaped, with formal gardens close to the manor giving way to grassy parkland punctuated by Himalayan pines, a dawn redwood native to China, and other exotic trees. Outdoor artworks include untitled limestone bas reliefs by E.B. Cox and *The Whole Person*, Lionel

Thomas's symbolic wall-mounted sculpture constructed of bronze plates and brass rods.

S E C R E T
GOLF

Hot on the heels of San Diego and Chicago, Toronto the green is the world's third-largest urban Mecca for tee worshipers. Boasting roughly 100 public courses within easy driving distance (by car, not by club), Toronto has enough undiscovered sand traps and water hazards to tempt even the most orthodox golfer from the straight and narrow.

Home of the Bell Canadian Open, Oakville's **Glen Abbey** (1333 Dorval, Oakville, 905-844-1811) is one of Canada's top-rated public golf courses and was designed by the legendary Jack Nicklaus. Non-members are welcome to golf at Glen Abbey, although you should book tee-off times at least six weeks in advance. A round of 18 holes will cost $125 to $230, depending on the day and season. While you're there, take a swing through the **Royal Canadian Golf Association Museum and Golf Hall of Fame** (416-849-9700), located inside a former Jesuit monastery.

Toronto Parks and Recreation operates five courses within city limits, each with its own pro shop and rental equipment. Prices range from $13 to $49 for an 18-hole round, according to the age of the golfer, the day of the week, and the course being played. The most central is the **Don Valley Golf Course** (4200 Yonge, north of Wilson, 416-392-2465), only a five-minute walk north from the York Mills subway.

Players must stroll back and forth under the Highway 401 overpass, but there's no danger of having to retrieve wayward balls from the middle of the autobahn. Laid out in a classic Howard Watson design, the Don Valley course is a fairly difficult par 71, and the natural setting (if you ignore the highway) is quite pretty. Opened in 1967, the pitch-and-putt **Dentonia Park Golf Course** (781 Victoria Park, at Danforth, 416-392-2558) is situated on part of the farm estate created by Walter Massey in 1897 and named after his wife, Susan Marie Denton. The par-70 **Humber Valley Golf Course** (40 Beattie, north of Wilson and east of Islington, 416-392-2488) presents a challenging combination of links and valley holes laid out along the Humber River. **Scarlett Woods Golf Course** (1000 Jane, at Eglinton West, 416-392-2484) is an executive-length par 62, while the **Tam O'Shanter Golf Course** (2481 Birchmount, north of Sheppard, 416-392-2547), located on Highland Creek in the northeast corner of Metro, is a moderately difficult par 70.

S E C R E T

GOTHIC

The fashionable late-18th-century revival of Gothic architecture, with its distinctive spires and pointed arches, found expression in several Toronto structures. The oldest is **Little Trinity Church** (425 King East, east of Parliament, 416-367-0272), completed in 1845. Designed by Henry Bowyer Lane, the building boasts a crenellated tower and octagonal corner buttresses, among other delights. The

nearby **Rectory** (417 King East) is Georgian by design but sports a few Gothic details.

Built in Gothic Revival style by a successful local brewer, to benefit children of the area's Protestant Irish working class, the **Enoch Turner Schoolhouse** (106 Trinity Street, 416-863-0010) was constructed in 1848 on the grounds of Little Trinity Church. The schoolhouse survived many interim uses — serving as a Boer War recruiting center, a Depression-era soup kitchen, and a Sunday school, among other things — before being restored in the 1970s as an education museum, with period artifacts and a research library. The schoolhouse is often the site of fashion shows, seasonal fairs, and other public events and is open for free tours by appointment only, between 10 a.m. and 4 p.m. year round.

After the Great Fire of 1849 destroyed the third church built on the same site, the seriously Gothic **Cathedral Church of St. James** (106 King East, at Church, 416-364-7865) was erected with a 306-foot tower and spire — Canada's tallest and North America's second tallest (after St. Patrick's in New York). Inside, take a look at the turn-of-the-century stained glass window by New York's Tiffany & Co., the impressive hammer-beam ceiling, and the marbled apsidal chancel where the influential Bishop John Strachan is laid to rest. The grand organ, handsomely housed in Queen Anne cases, has nearly 5,000 individual pipes, and the cathedral regularly serves as a choral concert venue for various local groups, including the **Orpheus Choir of Toronto** (416-530-4428).

Perhaps the prettiest example of Gothic architecture is the **Toronto Necropolis Chapel** (200 Winchester, 416-923-7911), constructed in 1872 on the city's 18-acre nonsectarian burial ground. The High Victorian Gothic embellishments include fancy ironwork, complex tracery, and a colorfully decorative slate roof.

SECRET

GOTHS

Toronto is home to a thriving counterculture of young men and women with preternaturally pale skin and dark clothes — the local goth community, estimated to exceed several thousand members and most visible in the Queen West district. A number of local goth-positive clubs offer sanctuary at night, not to mention cocktails and conducive tunes.

Retro/goth/industrial music is favored on Friday and Saturday nights at **Savage Garden** (550 Queen West, at Bathurst, 416-504-2178). The club also hosts occasional "masquerade interactive role-playing" nights. Other clubs with regular goth nights include **Velvet Underground** (510 Queen West, 416-504-6688), decorated in metal and velvet and boasting a large dance floor, **Area 51** (577 King West, 416-977-4036), and **Vatikan** (1032 Queen West, 416-533-9166), a new club run by the former proprietor of the now-defunct Sanctuary Vampire Sex Bar. **Anarchist's Cocktail** (1286 Bloor West, east of Lansdowne, 416-536-5341), where they spin goth, industrial, techno, synthpop, and retro sounds, opens at 10 p.m., and there's never a cover charge.

If your wardrobe is lacking the requisite black apparel, drop by **Siren Alternative Clothing and Accessories** (463 Queen West, 416-504-9288), where proprietors Morpheus and Groovella have been outfitting local goths for more than a decade. The nearby **House of Ill Repute** (469 Queen West, 416-203-0170) carries Victorian, Gothic, and fetish fashions and accessories, mostly for women. Owner/designer Gwyn Strang stresses PVC and lace (though not necessarily together). Designer dungeon wear by Pam Chorley, who has a predilection for velvet, is available from **Fashion Crimes** (395 Queen West, 416-592-9001), while leather shackles, studded collars, and other accessorizing bondage gear can be acquired at **He and She Clothing Gallery** (263 Queen East, 416-594-0171). For a custom-made corset, contact Diana DiNoble, who runs a private downtown studio called **Starkers!** (416-871-1675). She also creates a full range of darkly romantic dresses and a few black hats.

S E C R E T

GROUP OF SEVEN

Built in Byzantine style in 1907, featuring a great dome, **St. Anne's Anglican Church** (651 Dufferin, north of Dundas West, 416-536-3160) recruited 10 artists in 1923 to decorate the interior, and the result is one of Toronto's most colorful churches. Three of the chosen painters were members of the recently formed Group of Seven — J.E.H. MacDonald had the contract, and he hired F.H. Varley and Frank Carmichael to help out — but don't expect to see familiar windswept Canadian landscapes, because the artwork conforms to the church aesthetic. (For the essential collection of Group of Seven works, you'll need to drive north of the city to the **McMichael Canadian Art Collection** in Kleinburg, 905-893-1121.) Other artists included Frances Loring and Florence Wyle, who contributed the sculptural reliefs. The church has been designated as a national historic site. The regular service at St. Anne's takes place every Sunday at 10 a.m., and visitors can linger afterwards for a closer look at the interior decoration. A descriptive brochure is available at the church. Another opportunity arises every third Sunday at 4:30 p.m., when St. Anne's offers choral evensong. The building is locked during the week, but special tours can be arranged for groups of 10 or more by calling the church office. The church is also a concert venue — scheduled events are published in *WholeNote* (see "Other Resources").

MacDonald's decorative skills are also displayed at the **Concourse Building** (100 Adelaide West, 416-368-4262), a 16-story Art Deco skyscraper built in 1929. The elaborate tile mosaic gracing the arched entranceway was designed by him and his son, Thoreau MacDonald. Airplanes, stylized eagles, sailing ships, furnaces, and other images symbolize the "concourse" of elements (fire, earth, air, and water). The upper walls of the lobby were originally decorated with quotations from Canadian poetry, carved into the surface and gilded, but that embellishment has since been lost.

Still standing at the south end of the Rosedale ravine, behind the Canadian Tire building at Yonge and Davenport, is the **Studio Building** (Severn Street, off Aylmer just west of Park Road). Funded in part by Group of Seven member Lawren Harris (although the group did not yet exist as such), the three-story structure features open studio floors and tall windows facing north for the proper light. Completed in 1914, it was the first building in Canada designed and built specifically as a studio space for artists — Harris, J.E.H. MacDonald, and A.Y. Jackson were among the first occupants — and it contributed in its own way to the momentum of the new artistic movement.

S E C R E T
HIKING

The ravines and valleys snaking through Toronto's urban core, as well as the natural and machine-made features of the Lake Ontario waterfront, provide numerous opportunities to stretch your legs and commune with nature. Don't forget to prepare for your hike: take a hat and sunscreen, wear long pants and sturdy shoes, bring along a jacket or rain gear just in case, and pack a water bottle, lunch or a snack, and a map of the area, if one is available.

The **Humber River Valley** trail is pretty much paved from end to end, and popular with cyclists, although there are several dirt-path detours through the wooded sections. It traces part of a historic trading route, the main north-south artery connecting Lake Ontario to the Holland River — a 48-kilometer (30-mile) portage! — until Lieutenant-Governor John Graves Simcoe cleared Yonge Street in 1796. The bottom third of today's trail, from the lakeshore (where it connects with the Martin Goodman Trail) north to Bloor Street, offers a few glimpses of the Humber Marsh. But the best place to start is at the Old Mill subway (walk east from the station along Bloor, to the huge bridge that reaches over the valley, and take the wooden steps that lead down into the ravine). The route north, starting at the ruins of William Gamble's 1848 sawmill, takes you through Étienne Brulé Park, shady Lambton Woods, the formal James Gardens, and Scarlett Mills Park. North of Eglinton, the trail continues through Ukrainian Canadian Memorial Park and ends at Raymore Park, where 1954's infamous Hurricane Hazel caused the Humber to swell and carry away 36 residents of Raymore Drive. (The southbound Scarlett 79 bus, from the stop at Raymore and Scarlett Road, will take you to the Runnymede subway.)

Numerous city groups arrange walking trips. Representatives from **Toronto Parks and Recreation** (416-392-8186) lead a series of outdoor walks, from bird-watching and spring garden tours to heritage site visits and fall color parades. The **Task Force to Bring Back the Don** (416-392-0401) also hosts a full schedule of walking tours, designed to highlight the natural splendor and current degradation of the Don River Valley as part of the group's ongoing campaign to revive Toronto's long-neglected waterway. Similarly, the **Toronto Field Naturalists** (416-593-2656) attempt to stimulate public interest in natural history and encourage the preservation of our natural heritage through numerous free outings. Single nature lovers are encouraged to pursue outdoor pleasures in the company of others, on group walks arranged by **A Stroll in the Park** (416-969-3162; recorded information 484-9255). Afternoon walks and weekend adventures take place year round — call for prices and dates.

SECRET
HISTORY

Fort Rouillé, a wooden-walled trading post built in the winter of 1750 by the Marquis de la Jonquière, marked the first European settlement at what is now Toronto. The spot today is marked by an unassuming stone monument, located at the southwest corner of Exhibition Place. Not far to the east, the British-built **Fort York**

(100 Garrison, at the foot of Bathurst, 416-392-6907) stands back from the harbor. Over time, the Lake Ontario shoreline has moved away from the fortress enclosure, earthen walls that once supported log palisades. The fort was torched by American troops in 1813 — and the muddy town of York was duly sacked — but the rebuilt blockhouses, officers' quarters, and stone-walled powder magazine now house a busy little heritage industry: costumed interpreters reenact military drills with cannons and muskets, while kitchen staffers bake bread and cookies. Guided tours are available, and there's free parking too.

The Canadian military used the fort until 1930, although the troops saw little action. In 1837 they were called out to quell the Upper Canada Rebellion led by William Lyon Mackenzie, who fled to the United States. After being pardoned, he returned to resume his public life — he had been elected Toronto's first mayor in 1834. Mackenzie's last home, a gas-lit Victorian rowhouse just two blocks east of today's Eaton Centre, has been restored by the Toronto Historical Board as a museum and gallery. **Mackenzie House** (82 Bond, 416-392-6915) comes complete with costumed staff and a fully functional, 19th-century print shop, much like the one Mackenzie used to publish his rabble-rousing newspapers.

A rare survivor from the original town of York, the restored **Campbell House** (160 Queen West, at University, 416-597-0227) was built in 1822 but initially stood on nearby Adelaide Street. The first owner of this Georgian home was a former chief justice of Upper Canada, Sir William Campbell. Period decor (though not the original furniture) graces the interior, there's a model of the Town of York circa 1825, and costumed interpreters lead tours and demonstrate 19th-century domestic life.

More evidence of earlier times exists at **Colborne Lodge** (Colborne Lodge Drive, south end of High Park, near the Queensway, 416-392-6916), a picturesque 1830s Regency-style cottage with many of its original furnishings. The former home of Jemima and John George Howard was donated to the city in 1873, along with High Park itself. Howard was one of the city's first architects, as well as an artist and engineer. Still in its original parkland setting, Colborne Lodge has not suffered the usual encroachment of modern construction. The lodge is open in the afternoons, as well as on special occasions. To get there, take the 501 Humber streetcar on Queen Street, or walk south through the park from the Bloor Street entrance near the High Park subway.

Located about a mile north of Sheppard, the **Gibson House Museum** (5172 Yonge, 416-395-7432) was truly in the boondocks when it was built in 1851 — and many downtowners still consider this area the outer reaches. In fact, it's not too far from the towers of the North York Civic Centre and Mel Lastman Square (named after a man with an edifice complex, who later became the megacity's first mayor). The 10-room museum was the residence of David and Elizabeth Gibson and their seven children. David Gibson was a land surveyor, farmer, and local politician whose support for the unsuccessful Rebellion of 1837 led to the burning down of his original home on this site. Tours, domestic demonstrations, and a full program of workshops, craft sales, and seasonal celebrations — including Christmas and Hogmanay — are offered, and the bookstore stocks titles with a historical focus for both kids and adults.

Toronto's oldest building is **Scadding Cabin** (Exhibition Place), built in 1794 by John Scadding, friend and clerk to Upper Canada's first lieutenant-governor, John Graves Simcoe. It originally stood on Scadding's property east of the Don River — at Queen Street (then known as Kingston Road), just about where the Don Valley Parkway now runs — but was moved to its present site in time for the opening of the first Canadian National Exhibition in 1879.

The **Heritage Toronto Resource Centre** (205 Yonge, 416-392-6827) resides in the restored 1906 Bank of Toronto, designed by Toronto architect E.J. Lennox. His miniature Pantheon is the site of ongoing celebrations of this city's past, with a lecture series, workshops, and temporary exhibits. The center also sells a few books about Toronto history and a set of walking tour pamphlets.

SECRET
HOME
ENTERTAINMENT

The technology of home entertainment evolves at a rapid pace, and the classy equipment that disappears from rec rooms and shop windows shortly after the new models arrive is soon ancient history. Peter Campbell and Keith Maitland, owners of stereo store **Reid and Campbell Limited** (2013 Yonge, between Davisville and Eglinton, 416-483-3553), recognized the trend and decided to start rescuing these audiovisual artifacts. Their private collection of early TVs, radios, tape players, and phonographs consists mainly of stuff sold in Canada, dating back to when the store first opened in 1933, although they own a few earlier items, such as a circa-1915 Edison wax-cylinder phonograph. Other highlights include a Sony Trinitron from 1969, when the model was first introduced in Canada, and an early Betamax video player. The collection is not always on display, so if you plan to visit call first to make sure there's something to see.

Vintage audiophiles will also appreciate **Ring Audio Service** (1860 Queen East, near Woodbine, 416-693-7464), where the specialty is rejuvenating old equipment. The store has a small display of jukeboxes, Bakelite radios, and old stereos, guaranteed to induce a fit of nostalgia.

S E C R E T
HUNGARIAN

I swear, **The Coffee Mill** (99 Yorkville, 416-920-2108) must be a regular stop on some Yorkville bus tour for the blue-rinse set. Every lunch hour during the week, the place is packed, and there's no one under 60. Since it's hidden away on the ground floor of a mini-mall and not visible from the street, you probably wouldn't find The Coffee Mill unless you were looking. But it's been around long enough to achieve institutional status, and fans know how to find it. When it opened in 1963, in a now-vanished Yorkville location closer to Bloor Street, it claimed a little fame as a pioneer, being Toronto's first European-style sidewalk café. Al fresco drinking and dining were unheard of — illegal, in fact — until the early 1960s, and owner Martha von Heczey was first to take advantage of the relaxed regulations. Unlike the many cramped and car-fumed patios that now cling to the curb elsewhere in Yorkville, The Coffee Mill's secluded courtyard is cool and shady, with lots of elbow room. The menu has changed very little in 40 years, featuring chunky goulash soup, wiener schnitzel, veal paprikash with spaetzle, mounds of mashed potatoes and red cabbage, daily specials (including chicken soup with liver dumplings, available only on Saturday), and sweet, spiked coffees.

At one time, a quest for cabbage rolls in Toronto led invariably to the Annex, where Hungarian home cooking was available at a handful of Bloor Street diners. Alas, those venerable eateries have now given way to a string of sushi bars, and the neighborhood is no longer referred to as Little Budapest. The last holdout is **Country Style** (450 Bloor West, 416-537-1745), where you can still order a heaping helping of two large, meaty rolls, caressed with sour cream and accompanied by boiled potatoes and rye bread. The strudel is nothing to sneer at either.

A strip of beach and green space along Lake Ontario called **Budapest Park** (Lakeshore Boulevard West, west of Jameson) is the site of a monument, by Hungarian-born artist Victor Tolgesy, commemorating the 10th anniversary of the Hungarian uprising of 1958.

SECRET

ICE CREAM

Tucked in several steps below street level, just across Bloor from the Royal Ontario Museum, **Greg's Ice Cream** (200 Bloor West, 416-961-4734) serves up scoops of all-natural homemade frozen stuff. There are flavors enough to tingle anyone's taste buds, from white chocolate to green tea, and you can dress them up with sprinkled nuts, pureed strawberries, or hot fudge topping (among other delights).

During the summer months, long lineups stretch out the door of **Dutch Dreams** (78 Vaughan, just north of St. Clair, 416-656-6959), a charming little corner shop decorated on the outside with an assortment of ice cream cones and Dutch figures. Inside, the homemade ice cream is dished out by the cone or the carton. Grape nut is the most popular flavor with the local Jamaican clientele. Dutch Dreams also stocks fine mineral water and a small selection of imported licorice — the traditional salty kind, including the toffee-colored salmiak that tastes slightly of ammonia. You can enjoy Dutch waffles and pancakes, fresh-fruit frozen yogurts, and other desserts at one of the half-dozen tables in the little raised dining area at the back of the shop or outside on the bench in summer. Bring your sweetheart and your sweet tooth.

For exquisite hazelnut gelato, there's no better place than the **Sicilian Ice Cream Company** (712 College, 416-531-7716), where you can park yourself indoors or out and savor it from a silver dish. Of course, it's even better if you add a second scoop of chocolate or vanilla or . . . buy it by the kilo and take it home. Another traditional favorite is **La Paloma Gelateria and Café** (1357 St. Clair West, 416-656-2340), where customers appreciate the wide choice of flavors and authentic recipes from Italy. On hot summer evenings, the lineup can stretch double the length of this narrow shop, but the young cone-jockeys work hard to keep things moving, so don't be discouraged. Besides, you'll need the extra time just to make a decision.

At numerous shops around town, you can buy small tubs of ice cream and sorbet made by **Gelato Fresco** (60 Tycos, 416-785-5415), but why not go straight to the source? The retail outlet near Dufferin and Lawrence has a sit-down gelateria, where you can try out all the flavors, including seasonal batches. Order an Illy espresso on the side, or have it poured hot into a cold vanilla milkshake.

Exotic flavors like lychee, sea moss with oatmeal, saffron, soursop, and others are the stock in trade at **Tropical Treets** (130 Bermondsey, 416-759-8777). For over 10 years, this family business has been making sorbet, ice cream, and Indian kulfi for restaurants and ethnic grocers across Canada. Now you can sit down at the main shop and choose from close to 100 varieties of frozen treats.

SECRET
IMPORTS

Block-printed Indian tablecloths, Bangladeshi cane baskets and handmade gilded stationery, carved bookends and stone soap dishes from Kenya, and traditional Zimbabwean mbira (thumb pianos) are among the many colorful products sold at **Bridgehead** (18 Roy's Square, southeast of Yonge and Bloor, 416-975-8788). While similar objects can be found elsewhere, the difference here is that Bridgehead (the retail arm of Oxfam Canada) operates with a deliberate policy of fair trade, paying fair prices directly to creative artisans, small family workshops, and nonprofit co-ops. By cutting out the middleman, Bridgehead supports impoverished communities in Third World countries. Ten years ago, its main import was Nicaraguan coffee beans. You can still buy coffee, including blends from Costa Rica and even instant coffee from Tanzania, but Bridgehead's trading horizons have expanded considerably to include everything from clothing for adults and children to the BayGen Freeplay radio — an innovative and award-winning radio designed to play without batteries or electricity (it runs on its own wind-up generator). Manufactured in Cape Town,

South Africa, by a company that treats its employees with dignity, the BayGen radio is endorsed by Nelson Mandela and more than 20 international humanitarian organizations.

S E C R E T
INDIAN

More than a dozen sari-and-silk shops vie for attention within the crowded five or six blocks comprising **Little India** (Gerrard East, between Highfield and Coxwell). The largest dedicated store is **Maharani Fashions** (1417 Gerrard East, 416-466-8400), while nearby **Sangam Silk Store** (1421 Gerrard East, 416-466-4213) and **Sonu Saree Palace** (1420 Gerrard East, 416-469-2800) offer exquisite silk bargains. This bustling neighborhood is the center of Toronto's silk and spice trade, especially on Sunday, when families are out on parade in their silken best. The brightly lit storefronts and year-round holiday lights add to the festive air. While you're shopping, don't miss **Milan's Department Store** (1460 Gerrard East, 416-461-1456), a veritable bazaar of imported East Indian fashions, stainless-steel culinary vessels, religious statuettes, jewelry, musical instruments, and colorful saris. Indian sweets are also available here, but the best selection can be found at **Surati Sweet Mart** (1407 Gerrard East, 416-462-3480). Among the many varieties, the little square or diamond-shaped burfi is distinctive for its blend of rosewater, pistachio, and cardamom, sometimes decorated with silver leaf. The friendly staff at Surati will happily help the uninitiated assemble a variety pack of brightly colored sponges and sweets.

The **Indian Record Shop** (1428 Gerrard East, 416-463-6671) is the spot for CDs and tapes of Indian and Pakistani music, from popular and classical to religious. It also stocks a good selection of Indian videos. Translations of the Koran and other Muslim texts, both secular and religious, can be purchased at **Islamic Books and Souvenirs** (1395 Gerrard East, 416-778-8461), along with additional religious paraphernalia.

If you need a snack to sustain your shopping energy, the **Madras Express Café-Dosa** (1438-A Gerrard East, 416-461-7470) is a good stop for pani puri, savory puffed-up wafers filled with spiced chickpeas, potato, and piquant tamarind juice or variations on the theme. The Express also serves masala dosa, a popular breakfast meal made of feather-light rice-and-lentil crepes filled with deliciously spiced potato and onion, accompanied here by coconut sauce and a small bowl of lentil soup.

For an inexpensive Indian meal, usually in the $6 to $8 range, try **Madras Durbar** (1435 Gerrard East, 416-465-4116), which offers an entirely vegetarian menu of spicy South Indian cuisine, or the **Skylark** (1433 Gerrard East, 416-469-1500) for buffet specials. The **Moti Mahal Restaurant** (1422 Gerrard East, 416-461-3111) is also a good choice for vegetarian specialties, and their samosas are the best on the block. Don't let the low-budget decor fool you. Nonvegetarians may prefer the **Shan-E-Hind Bar-be-que Hut** (1455 Gerrard East, 416-466-2264), which does great tandoori dishes, offers tongue-cooling saffron ice cream for dessert, and entertains with live traditional music on weekends.

After a meal, when hands and mouth have been washed, it is often customary to finish up with a little paan: betel nuts, lime, and sweet spices wrapped in betel leaf. Several shops in Little India, including

Baldev Pan Cold Drink House (1399 Gerrard East, 416-463-7226), sell paan, as do most Indian and Pakistani grocery stores.

SECRET
INFOMERCIALS

Anyone with a fondness for late-night infomercials has heard the refrain "Not sold in stores!" It's meant to convince insomniac shopaholics that the amazing gadget revealed on screen is a unique treasure, available exclusively to those lucky few (thousands of) viewers who heed the hawker's advice to pick up the phone and "Call now!" Putting the lie to that popular pitch — albeit without a trace of irony — **As Seen on TV Showcase** (Dufferin Mall, 900 Dufferin, 416-536-5551, plus three other Toronto locations) lets you buy those coveted products in person. Now you can walk in during regular daylight hours and browse the showroom for all your favorite slicing and dicing kitchen contraptions (the Starfrit potato chipper, for example, or the Sushi Master kit, complete with nonstick sushi knife), chemical hair-removers, massage rollers, Chia pets, and exercise equipment for fabulous abs and a firmer butt (including the ever-popular Suzanne Somers's Toning System). Wall-mounted television sets replay the original commercials, while store staff are happy to give live demonstrations. All products in the store are pretested and approved for sale by the parent company, so you won't find some of the more dubious devices advertised on TV. The concept behind this popular franchise is to remove the barriers put up by the TV-only experience — in-store shoppers can try before they buy, avoid giving their credit card number over the phone, and not worry about hidden shipping and handling charges. Plus, you enjoy the somewhat surreal experience of stepping into a live infomercial. This is reality TV of a different sort.

S E C R E T
IRISH

Got a favorite Irish rugby squad? You can probably find a team shirt at **Irish Traditions** (444 Yonge, in College Park, 416-977-7917). The shop carries a collection of Celtic jewelry — you can even order custom-designed claddagh engagement and wedding bands — Belleek china (a pearly, translucent porcelain first produced in the Northern Irish town of that name), the cheaper and very green Knock pottery, music, books, CDs, and other Hibernian gear. Or, if you like scratchy woolens designed for the bogs and moors but suitable for damp Toronto days, visit the **Irish Shop** (150 Bloor West, 416-922-9400).

Looking for somewhere authentically Irish to imbibe a pint of Guinness? Head on over the Bloor Street Viaduct to **Dora Keogh** (141 Danforth, east of Broadview, 416-778-1804), a country pub with bench-and-stool seating around copper-topped tables, a stone fireplace, home cooking from Yer Ma's Kitchen, and, of course, a long bar running half the length of the room. On Thursday evenings and late Sunday afternoons, musicians gather for a session of traditional Irish tunes. Sláinte!

SECRET
ITALIAN

In 1976, the Italian consulate in Toronto established the **Istituto Italiano di Cultura** (496 Huron, north of Bloor, 416-921-3802) as a center for cultural and academic initiatives, including Italian language classes, film and video screenings, and art exhibitions. During my first visit to the institute, I was charmed by a display of utterly eccentric furniture designed by Carlo Bugatti — an exotic mélange of animal skins, ebony, inlays, and tassels — and charmed as well by the custodian's enthusiastic personalized tour.

Local residents, law enforcement officials, and even well-known hockey players line up for the veal on a kaiser at **California Sandwiches** (244 Claremont, one block north of Dundas, 416-603-3317). Take your pick of sweet, medium, or hot, with mushrooms or cheese — extra onions are free — and place your order at the take-out counter. There's a brightly painted blue-and-yellow indoor eating area, but if you'd rather eat alfresco walk a few blocks west on Dundas to the open green space of Trinity Bellwoods Park (see "Secret Parks").

Gio's (2070 Yonge, north of Davisville, 416-932-2306) has absolutely no standing room in the narrow entranceway. Employees sometimes send patrons a few doors up the road to wait in the front area of a second restaurant, called **Five Doors North** (2088 Yonge, 416-480-6234). The trouble is, neither restaurant bears a name out front: instead of a lettered sign, Gio's has a humongous nose hooked above the door, and Five Doors North still has the Future Furniture sign from the previous occupant. Inside, Five Doors North has an eclectic decor, to say the least: a confessional booth sitting to one side, near the large open kitchen; a small collection of film-editing equipment perched on a low wall; lighting comprising cheesy table lamps suspended from the ceiling with metal strapping; and a few paintings that came from the same garage sale as the lamps. Somehow, it works. And the food, at both restaurants, is fabulous (not to mention surprisingly well priced): traditional multicourse meals might include fritelle and grilled zucchini appetizers, pasta with butternut squash sauce, a mixed seafood plate, grilled lamb, rich portobello mushrooms and full-flavored rapini, followed by exquisite crème caramel.

S E C R E T
JAMAICAN

Don't leave town without trying Albert Wiggan's amazing chicken curry, served on rice and beans with a side of coleslaw. The kitchen at **Albert's Real Jamaican Foods** (542 St. Clair West, at Vaughan, 416-658-9445) has more space than the customer side of the counter, where there are only a few stools for sitting along the window, but the friendly service and good music will put you in an island mood you can carry away with your take-out food. Roti, cod fritters, jerk dinners, and braised oxtail stew are also on the menu.

Vegetarian pepper pot soup, jerk chicken salad with avocado and mango, and red snapper with banana dumplings betray the culinary expertise of the chefs at **Irie** (808 College, east of Ossington, 416-531-4743). This is no ordinary Jamaican eatery, despite the palm fronds and requisite posters of the legendary Bob Marley. Dinners, including the highly recommended jerk pork, are accompanied by thyme-and-garlic-spiced coconut rice and peas. And watch out for the full-strength peppers. If your throat needs cooling, ask for a bottle of Red Stripe beer, or sample the fresh-fruit punch (with or without a jigger of island rum). Better yet, try the "steel bottom," a relaxing concoction of beer and rum.

The population of Toronto's Caribbean community exceeds 300,000, making this the world's third-largest Caribbean city (after Kingston, Jamaica, and Havana, Cuba). That fact is unsurprising to anyone who's been in town at the end of July and early August, when the air is alive with steel drum bands and island crooners celebrating Caribana, the city's biggest cultural festival. While most of the frol-icking takes place downtown, the uptown stretch of Eglinton Avenue West between Marlee and Keele (starting just a few blocks west of the Eglinton West subway and extending south along Oakwood and Vaughan) is where the real community — informally known as **Little Jamaica** — resides. Here, a hubbub of record stores, roti shops, and various other businesses catering to the local Caribbean community merges with the area's older Italian and Portuguese roots to offer a vibrant neighborhood blend of everything from Rasta to pasta.

SECRET
JAPANESE

Catering to the Japanese community since 1968, **Sanko Trading Co.** (730 Queen West, at Claremont, 416-703-4550) carries everything you need to make sushi at home, except fresh fish. You can pick up high-quality sushi rice, as well as the requisite wasabi — a hot green paste made from horseradish root — in powdered form or premixed in tubes. The shelves are stocked with spices, Japanese vegetables, imported soy sauce and numerous other sauces, plus staples such as miso, nori (seaweed), and umeboshi (pickled plums, traditionally eaten at breakfast, that aid digestion by keeping the intestinal tract clear, if you know what I mean). Sanko also carries Japanese cutlery, serving dishes, woven baskets, Kokeshi dolls, and a wide variety of colorfully packaged candy, including Pokemon gum and Hello Kitty products. One of the most popular treats is Gilco pocky, a chocolate-covered breadstick that reportedly gets its name from the "pocky" sound it makes when snapped in half. For a more traditional snack, try the rice crackers or the surume (dried cuttlefish).

Papermaking is one of many Japanese arts, and the best place to find beautiful handmade washi is the **Japanese Paper Place** (887 Queen West, 416-703-0089). Here you'll find opaque patterned papers, tissue-like obonai feather papers, watermark papers, silk-screened kozo papers that mirror kimono designs, papers printed with kanji script, and numerous other varieties. Owner Nancy Jacobi, who opened the store in 1982, keeps up with the industry and in touch with suppliers by making an annual pilgrimage to various papermaking villages in Japan. While the entire stock is represented here at the main store, fine artists can drool (figuratively speaking, please) over full sheets at the **Japanese Paper Place Warehouse** (79 Brock, by appointment only, 416-538-9669). Occasional exhibits take place in a space upstairs at the back of the warehouse, as do regular weekend workshops on such topics as lamp-making, bookbinding, photo transfer to paper, box-making, card-making, paper-dyeing, and so on. You can register by phone or in person at the store.

Unlike other ethnic groups, the Japanese community occupies no particular area of town, so there's no Little Japan to seek out for sushi and sake. Sushi bars have recently come back into vogue, however, popping up like mushrooms in the Annex and along Queen Street West, and several reliable restaurants have been around for years. One of my favorites is **Ematei** (30 St. Patrick, 416-340-0472), especially at lunchtime when the spectacular sushi special is even more affordable. Miso soup is a staple at any Japanese eating place, but for something a little different try Ematei's konchi tsuboyaki, a delicate conch broth with shiitake mushroom, served from the shell. Self-deprecating **Restaurant Rikishi** (833 Bloor West, at Shaw, 416-538-0760) is easy to miss, hidden behind paper screens on an otherwise unremarkable stretch of Bloor Street. Fresh sushi, sunomono, and other traditional dishes are served in tranquil surroundings.

SECRET
JUDAICA

A permanent display of Judaica and artifacts representing Jewish life in Toronto — religious objects, personal belongings, photographs, and other historical records — can be viewed at the **Silverman Heritage Museum** (Baycrest Centre for Geriatric Care, 3560 Bathurst, main floor, 416-785-2500, ext. 2802). Originally called the Toronto Jewish Old Folks' Home, the Baycrest Centre has been operating since 1918. The collection features religious artifacts such as Torah crowns, menorahs, Torah pointers, breastplates, and prayer books, all from around the turn of the century. The museum also offers activities tied to holiday celebrations, Jewish art, and local history.

Artifacts at the **Beth Tzedec Reuben and Helene Dennis Museum** (1700 Bathurst, 416-781-3511, ext. 32) include textiles, artworks, and more than 1,000 ceremonial objects. Dedicated to preserving Jewish heritage and interpreting Jewish customs and synagogue rituals, the museum presents lectures and educational programs. Tours are available.

Several bookstores serve the Jewish community in north Toronto: **Israel's The Judaica Centre** (897 Eglinton West, near Bathurst, 416-256-1010), **Aleph Bet Judaica** (3453 Bathurst, 416-781-2133), and **Negev Book and Gift Store** (3509 Bathurst, 416-781-9356).

S E C R E T

JUICE BARS

You may feel like slipping into Birkenstocks and something tie-dyed after visiting **Juice for Life** (521 Bloor West, 416-531-2635, and a smaller café at 336 Queen West, 416-599-4442), where the food is free of animal by-products and the long juice menu occupies most of one wall behind the bar. A full choice of coffees is also available, but the myriad fruit and vegetable combinations offer a refreshing alternative to the caffeine fix. It's good for your conscience as well as your constitution.

S E C R E T
KENSINGTON MARKET

The friendly chaos of **Kensington Market** — consisting of several closely packed streets west of Spadina and south of College (Augusta, Baldwin, Kensington, St. Andrews, and Nassau) — has so far survived the misguided intentions of city planners, whose sterile visions of "urban renewal" would surely have sapped the area's vital energy. Established in the early 1900s by Jewish merchants, whose handcart businesses evolved into front-lawn stalls and eventually a full-fledged market, Kensington has continued to serve successive waves of newcomers to the city. As the Jewish community began migrating north and west in the 1940s and '50s, the market area absorbed the influx of postwar Hungarian, Italian, Portuguese, and Ukrainian immigrants, followed in the 1970s by the Chinese and later by Latin Americans, East and West Indians, Koreans, and Vietnamese. In the 1980s, retro clothing shops and import stores opened up next to the grocery stores, followed by cafés and funky nightclubs. Gone are the crates of live chickens, and retail density has been curbed, but the outdoor displays, distinctive sidewalk awnings, and essential market atmosphere remain.

For specific Kensington Market sites, see **My Market Bakery** ("Secret Bakeries"), **Moonbean Café** ("Secret Coffee Beans"), **La Palette** ("Secret French"), **Pizzabilities R Endless** ("Secret Pizza"), and "Secret Synagogues."

S E C R E T

KOREAN

The area referred to as Little Korea is concentrated along Bloor Street West, between Christie and Bathurst (but mostly west of Palmerston). Bakeries, jewelers, restaurants, travel companies, herb shops, half a dozen 24-hour cybercafés, and designer import stores attract busloads of Korean tourists during the summer. **Korean Central Market** (675 Bloor West, 416-516-8022), formerly an IGA, now sells a fabulous variety of Asian foods, including seaweed prepared with sesame and tubs of creamy green tea ice cream. As elsewhere in multiethnic Toronto, several cultures intermingle (see "Secret Latin American"), but **Clinton's Tavern** (693 Bloor West, 416-535-9541) is probably the only place you'll see a traditional tavern, with a log-cabin interior and hockey on the big screen, joined at the hip to a karaoke bar and Korean cocktail lounge.

Across the street, an unusual, hand-tended baking contraption is set up in the window of **Hodo Kwaja (Walnut Cake)** (656 Bloor West, 416-538-1208). A short conveyor assembly passes little batter-filled molds in front of the attendant, who patiently drops a shelled walnut into the center of each one before it moves along and drops into the deep fryer. The little walnut cakes cost just over a dollar per half-dozen, and you can take them home or eat them at one of the tables in the back of the bakery.

If you like everything in pastel pink and blue with little cartoon characters all over it, visit the glorious **Morning Glory** (620A Bloor West, 416-538-8876) for sparkly stickers, reams of stationery, pencil cases, lidded mugs, photo albums, origami kits, car air fresheners, and other gifts. Don't miss the curtained booth just inside the front door, where you can get a souvenir sticker photo.

Catering to homesick (or merely hungry) Korean students, a clutch of cheap eateries populates the south side of Bloor. They are mostly small and plain, and some have no trace of English on the menu. If you don't have a Korean interpreter, and you don't feel brave enough to order at random, then you might prefer the $10 all-you-can-eat special at **Hodori Korean Buffet Restaurant** (691 Bloor West, 416-537-0972). It's the only self-serve buffet on the strip, so you can plainly see what you're putting on your plate.

Most of the upscale, more established restaurants reside on the north side of Bloor. The owner of **Korean Village Restaurant** (628 Bloor West, 416-536-0290) was something of a TV "personality" in Korea before coming to Canada, and her restaurant has become a popular destination for visitors from the old country, as well as a favorite among locals.

Korea House (666 Bloor West, 416-536-8666) is perhaps the oldest Korean restaurant in Toronto, and it still boasts excellent traditional cuisine, such as bulgoki (thin slices of marinated beef, barbecued at your table) and cold noodle dishes, including spicy sweet-potato-and-buckwheat noodles with marinated skate wing, vegetables, and hard-cooked egg. The quality of any Korean restaurant can be measured by the assortment of side dishes, or panchan, that accompany the main course. Korea House offers some of the best, including acorn flour cake, cabbage and daikon kimchi, various seaweeds, spinach, and hand-picked wild vegetables.

More authentic fare is available just around the corner at **Mul Rae Bang-A** (3 Christie, 416-534-6833), located right next to the Christie subway entrance. Like many Korean restaurants, it offers Japanese sushi on its mixed menu, but stick to the traditional dishes — they're excellent.

Two more spots worth mentioning can be found at some distance from the Bloor and Christie epicenter of Korean culture. **Yummy Bar-B-Q Korean Food** (2340 Dundas West, 416-588-5158) is hidden in an unfriendly looking, fortress-like mall called The Crossways at the corner of Bloor West and Dundas West. Portions are huge and cheap, and the walls are covered with color photos illustrating everything on the menu. Park free in the underground lot, or call for takeout. And down on trendy Queen Street West, stylish **San** (676 Queen West, 416-214-9429) serves sizzling bi bim bap, a steamed-rice dish with beef, vegetables, and fried egg. Afterwards, cool off with a bowl of ginger ice cream.

For a historical fix of Korean culture, don't miss the gallery of Korean art at the **Royal Ontario Museum** (100 Queen's Park, 416-586-5549). The largest of its kind in North America, this 2,300-square-foot exhibition space was designed to evoke the natural beauty and energy of Korea's landscape and features a dynamic historical survey. The gallery is new, but the museum has been collecting Korean artifacts since 1910, four years before the ROM opened its doors to the public. On display are objects representing 8,000 years of Korean cultural achievement, from ceramic art to evidence of early printing technologies.

SECRET
LAMB

I like to cook, and I like to eat out. But anything I've mastered in the kitchen I'm loath to order from a menu. Why bother, when I can get it at home anytime, done the way I like it? When it comes to rack of lamb, however, I'm barely an apprentice. Happily, it's a staple entrée at numerous eateries around town. **Silver Spoon** (390 Roncesvalles, 416-516-8112) serves a fantastic mustard-, rosemary-, and thyme-encrusted rack of eight, perfectly pink inside, on a sautéed vegetable-and-starch mélange of red potato, eggplant, and shredded greens. It's the most expensive item but easily affordable at $22. Reserve ahead, because word is out about this elegant neighborhood restaurant, whose stylish menu is matched by a striped and curvy decor in cool blue-greens. Both food and fittings offer a welcome alternative to the standard Roncesvalles fare of Polish pierogies and red tablecloths. The rest of the menu is equally rewarding, with calamari and carpaccio appetizers, specials that range from arctic char to succulent swordfish steaks, and addictive desserts like Belgian chocolate mini-soufflé, hot from the oven. The signature touches at Silver Spoon are the namesake napkin rings, silver spoons bent over a pole in the kitchen and used to clasp the table linen, among other things.

SECRET
LATIN AMERICAN

El Pipil (267 Danforth, east of Broadview, 416-465-9625) sells hand-knit woolly things from Bolivia and Nepal, wall sconces and hanging lanterns, incense burners, imported jewelry, and goblets of Mexican glass. The store is small, but the selection is pleasing and turns over fast.

Empanadas, skewers of sea bass, homemade corn bread, and excellent salsa are a few of the Peruvian delights at the **Boulevard Café** (161 Harbord, at Borden, 416-961-7676). Ceramic-tiled tabletops and hand-knotted wall hangings add color to the warm decor, while the large, awning-covered patio is the perfect spot to consume a jug of fresh-fruit and red wine sangria on a summer evening.

Home-cooked Latin American fare at **Tacos El Asador** (690 Bloor West, 416-538-9747) includes tacos (both soft and crispy), tamales, quesadillas, and pupusas — plus vegetarian versions of each — as well as fresh tamarind juice and the unusual horchata, a sweet and cloudy drink made from rice, peanuts, sugar, vanilla, and water. Huevos for breakfast (although the doors don't actually open until noon) come with fried beans, plantain, cream or cheese, and a tortilla. Tacos El Asador, located kitty-corner from Clinton's Tavern (see "Secret Korean"), is a small but sunny spot, with yellow-painted walls and mini picnic tables.

Several other Latin American spots populate this predominantly Korean strip of Bloor West. **El Paso** (660-B Bloor West, 416-539-0913) stocks a variety of *articulos latino*: sweaters and blankets, pottery, a few baked goods, corn flour, and other dry goods for the kitchen. Among the latter are packages of Mexican-style hot chocolate: chunks of cocoa with almonds and cinnamon, meant to be blended with hot milk. El Paso also offers western boots and a boot repair service, as the painted plywood sign suggests. **Tropical Corner** (612 Bloor West, 416-534-6675) covers all the bases, selling cafeteria-style meals and fresh tropical fruit drinks, CDs and cassettes, and long-distance telephone calls, as well as tax return preparation and other financial services. Closer to Christie, **Rincón Hispano** (729 Bloor West, 416-533-8930) sells a much broader selection of Spanish music, as well as a few dubbed Hollywood and international videos.

Elsewhere, a few other outposts of Latin American culture are worth visiting. If you fancy hand-painted terracotta, you'll find an entire store full of it at **Terracotta House** (315 Danforth, 416-966-1698). **El Bodegón** (537 College, at Euclid, 416-944-8297) specializes in Peruvian/Latin cuisine. And **Margaritas** (14 Baldwin, 416-977-5525), squished into the short, lively row of small shops and restaurants on Baldwin Street just west of McCaul, has a tapas bar and serves authentic Mexican dishes. As the name suggests, they also mix margaritas, the lime juice and tequila concoction served in salt-rimmed glasses that makes southern vacations so relaxing. In summer, the teensy patio out front is a perfectly pleasant spot to sit with a cold green beverage — among the dozen or so varieties, I particularly recommend the caipiriña, a Brazilian specialty featuring aguardiente (or "flaming water") sloshing about in a vessel resembling a small fish bowl.

Salsa and merengue fans can flaunt it at **El Convento Rico** (750 College, east of Ossington, 416-588-7800), a basement nightclub that features a friendly dance floor, late-night drag shows after 1 a.m., and Latin dance lessons on Sunday at 9 p.m. Good fun, especially for groups. East of Bathurst, **El Rancho Restaurant** (430 College, 416-921-2752) offers Latin American cooking and, after the dinner hour, dancing at **Borinquen** nightclub.

SECRET
LAUNDROMATS

Instead of watching your laundry spin, why not amuse yourself with a wind-up tin robot walking in circles? **Splish Splash** (590 College, at Clinton, 416-532-6499) is a full-service laundromat — they even do alterations and dry cleaning — but you wouldn't know it from the window display. It looks more like a toy store at Christmas. Owner Joseph Winter stocks the front section of Splish Splash with a dazzling collection of classic wind-up toys: brightly colored replicas of merry-go-rounds, zeppelins, mice on wheels, and various other mobile mechanical creatures — even Godzilla spitting a mouthful of sparks.

SECRET

LAW AND ORDER

You can explore both historical and contemporary policing methods at the **Metropolitan Toronto Police Museum and Discovery Centre** (40 College, at Bay, 416-808-7020), located on the main floor of police headquarters. Open every day from 9 a.m. to 9 p.m., the lineup includes drunk driving and substance abuse exhibits, crime-solving paraphernalia, and touch-screen displays that illustrate the science of fingerprint identification and the unreliable nature of eyewitness reports. There's also a circa-1929 jail cell replica, a 1914 paddy wagon, and a modern squad car to sit in. Fun for families and free too. At the gift shop, you can buy lots of police stuff — including a nifty fingerprint kit — as convincing evidence of your visit. Outside on College Street, a bronze sculpture of a policewoman troweling granite blocks is one-third of a work by Toronto artist Eldon Garnet entitled *To Serve and Protect*. The other two sculptures are around the corner on Grenville Street.

The beautiful but forbidding black iron fence surrounding **Osgoode Hall** (116–38 Queen West, at University, 416-947-3300) gives the impression of a private estate, and passersby might understandably think it denotes a no-trespassing zone. But Osgoode is a public building, created to serve as headquarters for the Law Society of Upper Canada and now home to the province's highest court. The iron palisades were cast in a Toronto foundry from molds created in Scotland, and the oddly chambered gates were in fact designed to keep out unwanted intruders: wandering cows, an occasional problem on Toronto streets in the mid-1800s (rare now but undoubtedly still unwelcome). Osgoode Hall — named after William Osgoode, Ontario's first chief justice — consisted originally of just the small east wing, completed in 1832. Numerous subsequent additions and renovations resulted in today's aristocratic structure, fronted by classical temple columns and sporting a row of rooftop urns that might remind the discerning observer of the garden at Versailles. Visitors can explore the grand interior staircase, a renovated 1867 courtroom, stern portraits, and the noble library with its 40-foot vaulted ceiling and beautiful plasterwork. Free tours take place on weekdays during July and August, although the building is open year round. Architectural plans of Osgoode Hall and other documents from as early as 1797, along with photos, inactive Law Society records, and material relating to the legal profession, are housed at the **Law Society of Upper Canada Archives** (130 Queen West, 416-947-4041).

SECRET
LAWN BOWLS

With more than 11,000 lawn bowlers and 170 clubs, Ontario clearly has a strong affection for this sport. And you can dispense with the stereotypical image of seniors in white togs, practicing for retirement in Florida: the lawn-bowls crowd is growing younger and younger, while the clothing is colorfully casual (although formal tournaments may still require whites). Nor is the sport an undemanding pastime. In a typical three-game tournament, a player must walk between two and five miles, do more than 250 knee bends, and lift and deliver a three-pound ball well over 1,000 feet, with great accuracy, during the course of a hot summer day. Though you may be in good physical condition, caution is also advised because the sport can be addictive — a well-known fact that led King Henry VIII to ban the playing of lawn bowls (except, of course, by the wealthy, who could afford to spend all their time at play).

In Toronto, lawn bowls is a perfectly legal pastime for all classes, although club membership is often required to participate. **Lawn Bowls Ontario** (416-426-7179) keeps a complete list of affiliated clubs, as well as a tournament schedule. The outdoor season rolls out from May to October, weather permitting. **Kew Beach Lawn Bowling Club** (foot of Lee, south of Queen East, 416-694-4371), with two full greens, is one of several clubs owned by the City of Toronto. Lake Ontario breezes keep temperatures pleasant, but a clear view of the Beaches boardwalk and scantily clad bathers has been known to distract a few bowlers from their game. Open bowling takes place every afternoon, seven days a week (unless preempted by a tournament), and experienced bowlers visiting the club may be permitted to join in. Although it may not be the most riveting spectator sport, observers are welcome. (On Saturday and Sunday mornings, mallet-wielding croquet players converge on the club for a little ball-whacking — soft, flat-soled shoes are a must, so leave your heels and cleats at home.)

Nearby you'll find the **Balmy Beach Club** (foot of Beech, south of Queen East, 416-691-9962), a privately owned club with one of the loveliest bowling greens in the city. (The clubhouse bar is also a great place to sneak into for an inexpensive glass of cold draft beer.)

By the way, if you're trying the sport for the first time, don't be disturbed to discover that the ball seems defective and wobbles off course. A lawn bowl is deliberately biased — that is, it is manufactured as a spherical ball but not perfectly balanced. As it slows down from the toss, it attempts to find its true balance and is forced to curve off in that direction. Just a little something to keep the game interesting.

SECRET

LEATHER

Family-owned **Northbound Leather** (586 Yonge, just north of Wellesley, 416-972-1037) has been around, under various monikers, since the late 1960s and has become Toronto's preeminent supplier of fetish gear. The store actually has two entrances, a front door at 586 Yonge Street (where you'll encounter leather jackets, pants, skirts, belts, and other fashionable clothes), and a discreet alleyway door at 7 St. Nicholas Street for direct access to the fun stuff. Custom orders can be manufactured in the store's own factory. Northbound sponsors special fetish nights on the third Thursday of the month, when it takes over all three floors of the **Limelight** nightclub (250 Richmond West). The dress code is strictly enforced — denim and athletic wear are disallowed, in favor of leather, rubber, pvc, drag, lingerie, uniforms, and goth attire.

Doc's Leather and Harley Davidson Gear (726 Queen West, 416-504-8888) carries a line of saddlebags, tool pouches, and sissy bar bags for strapping onto your bike, as well as leather gear to strap onto your body. For the security conscious, Doc's delivers leg irons and thumb cuffs, plus a selection of billy clubs, nightsticks, and slappers.

Looking for somewhere to sport your new chaps? You'll find birds of a feather at **Black Eagle** (457 Church, 416-413-1219), a leather and denim cruise bar, where proper attire is de rigueur on Friday and Saturday nights. There's plenty of play space here, with three full-service bars (drink service, that is) on two levels, plus a rooftop patio (winterized with an army tent and a couple of heaters during the snowy months). Black Eagle is an s/m bar, so if you don't like to play rough keep your hankie hidden in your pocket to avoid sending the wrong signal. Safe play is encouraged, the equipment (including vertical and horizontal slings) is free to use, and theme nights are popular.

Denim and leather are in fashion at **Toolbox** (508 Eastern, at Morse, 416-466-8616), which also caters to bears (big furry guys), nudists, and bikers. Located in Simcoe House, one block south of Queen and one block east of Logan, Toolbox attractions include a large outdoor patio and a restaurant serving home-cooked meals and Sunday brunch — the only thing at the club that's *not* leathery. Upstairs, **Muther's Guest House** offers comfortable rooms by the night or by the week.

SECRET
LIGHTHOUSES

The **Gibraltar Point Lighthouse** (Toronto Islands), a limestone tower completed in 1809 and originally equipped with a whale-oil lamp, was one of the first to be built on the Great Lakes. J.P. Rademuller, the very first keeper, disappeared suddenly in 1815. The mystery has never been solved, although some believe he was murdered by soldiers from Fort York when he refused to share his liquor, and the discovery of skeleton bits nearby lends credence to the theory. The lighthouse is no longer in operation, but Rademuller's ghost reputedly haunts the old tower. Located near the southwest corner of Centre Island, the lighthouse is easily accessible from Lakeshore Avenue, which winds around the outer edges of the Toronto Islands. (For Toronto Island ferry schedules, call 416-392-8193. The terminal is located on Queen's Quay East, at the foot of Bay.)

Also no longer a beacon for passing ships, the **Queen's Wharf Lighthouse** (Fleet Street, at Lakeshore Boulevard West) was relocated from its lakeside post in 1929 to its present patch of green far from the water's edge. This small clapboard structure was designed in 1861 by Kivas Tully, architect of the much grander Trinity College on Queen West (now demolished).

SECRET
LUNCHES

If you're poking around the Royal Ontario Museum and feeling a bit peckish, you could visit the ground-floor cafeteria — or you could rise to the occasion by seeking out the famous Yukon Gold french fries served at the fourth-floor JK ROM (100 Queen's Park, 416-586-5578). Open only during lunch hour, this is the lair of Toronto chef Jamie Kennedy. Fancy frites (also available with steak) aren't the only treat: perhaps you'd prefer miso-marinated sea bass or the five-year-old-cheddar tart. Starters include smoked salmon or coarse country pâté with celery root salad and walnut tuile, while the sweet after-thoughts encompass apple chestnut tart with caramel ice cream or a homemade plum sorbet. Before resuming your rounds among the museum artifacts, why not perk yourself up with a cup of herbal tea?

Even though Yonge and Bloor is understood to be Toronto's primary intersection, the geographical center that defines and divides our urban map into east-west/north-south quarters, it's almost the last place one thinks of when looking for somewhere to lunch. If you happen to find yourself stranded at the crossroads with an empty stomach, however, seek out **Biryani House** (6 Roy's Square, 416-927-9340), a back-street take-out joint with delicious weekday specials. Served on a silver platter (well, I suppose it's actually tin, but what can you expect for six bucks?), the meal includes rice, salad, side servings of raita and daal, two vegetables, a pile of pappadum chips, and the special itself (chicken biryani, vegetable thali, or some similar dish). The regular menu offers a good choice of slightly more expensive curries, vegetarian selections, breads, sweet Indian desserts, and a half-dozen variations on the yogurt drink known as lassi (try the salted lassi for something different). The restaurant has expanded to include an indoor seating area, and during warm-weather months more plastic tables and chairs are set outside on the pavement. Originally a delivery lane, this back alley was converted by the city, during subway renovations, into the pedestrian-friendly Roy's Square Mews, home to a shoe-repair shop, a designer clothing boutique, and more than a dozen other small stores and restaurants.

For delicious variations on the traditional club sandwich, including blackened chicken or peameal bacon, head over to the retro-chic **Lakeview Lunch** (1132 Dundas West, 416-530-0871), a neighborhood diner that looks like a movie set. And speaking of movies, why not indulge yourself at out-of-the-way **Mildred Pierce** (99 Sudbury, south of Queen and Dovercourt, 416-588-5695), named for the famous 1945 Joan Crawford flick. Located in the southeast corner of a warehouse building (watch for the big Studio 99 signs painted on the wall, then head down the east-end driveway), overlooking the GO train tracks where they cross King Street, the restaurant is decorated inside with huge murals and diaphanous hanging curtains. The menu leans toward Mediterranean (appetizers include fabulous flatbread and warm chèvre wrapped in vine leaves), and the cooking deserves an Oscar.

S E C R E T

MAKEUP

It takes more than a little lipstick and eyeliner to make the stars look good on screen. And when it comes to less conventional faces in film and television — say, the Elephant Man, an extra in *Planet of the Apes*, and especially alien invaders — a makeup artist needs to know a few more tricks than you'll learn from a lunchtime cosmetics demonstration at The Bay. That's where **Complections International** (85 St. Nicholas, 416-968-6739) comes in. Since 1979, Nadia Brandler's makeup school has been training theater and film-industry hopefuls in such Hollywood skills as period hairstyling, wig-knotting and ventilating, prosthetics, animatronics, and special effects (or "spfx," as it's called in the biz). Students also learn the fundamentals of fashion makeup, including makeup for photo shoots and fashion runways. Courses vary in length from two weeks to eight months. Located in a renovated two-story brick building on what was once a back alley to Yonge Street, the school is immediately distinguished by the monsters peering out through the plate glass windows. The display of handiwork continues inside along the "walk of stars," where you can watch students at work in the prosthetics lab or examine a couple of previous homework assignments, complete with documentation explaining how the creatures were created. The ground floor also houses a well-stocked makeup store featuring more than 33,000 items, from glitter and blush to wigs and stick-on tattoos. A room at the back is available for private consultations and makeovers, if you feel the need to change your look. And don't worry; they do much prettier work than just alien scales and claws.

More beauty products are available a few blocks away in Yorkville, where celebrity spotting is a popular sport, especially in September during the annual Toronto International Film Festival. At PIR **Cosmetics, Special F/X and Salon** (25 Bellair, 416-513-1603), founded by film-industry makeup artists Franchie Pir and Joanna Black, you'll find the makeup and hair care brands most favored by the stars: Shu Uemura, Paula Dorf, I Nuovi, B. Kamins, wu, Philip B., and Linda Cantello, among others. Services include professional makeup lessons, eyebrow shaping, and hair cutting and coloring. The Exotic Escape Manicure Bar offers essential oil treatments, rose-petal hand baths, and nail-coloring sessions set to music from the Middle East, the Orient, or the West Indies. Prepare to be pampered.

S E C R E T

MAPS

Exploration House (18 Birch, at the Summerhill subway, 416-922-5153) is true to its name. An exploratory ramble through the cluttered small rooms of this Victorian hideaway, on a sedate midtown side street, is not unlike an expedition of discovery. The cartographer's imagination, a country unto itself, comes vividly into view as you contemplate the early maps and globes, antiquarian books, and scientific instruments of enigmatic origin. You may be overtaken by the impulse — shared by scientists, sea captains, and modern-day collectors alike — to gather specimens as mementos of your visit to this exotic shore. Owners Neil and Liana Sneyd have been dealing from this spot since 1977, though they've been in business since 1963. Exploration House is really several destinations in one. While the Map Room is the mainstay, various other rooms focus on marine, wildlife, and sporting arts. Marine arts include paintings and prints by major artists from the 16th century to the present, model ships, brass portholes, relics from sunken wrecks, whaling memorabilia, and some fascinating pieces of scrimshaw — works etched into or carved from whalebone by sailors. Exploration House is open Tuesday to Saturday, 11 a.m. to 5:30 p.m., or by appointment.

Antique views of the world are on display at **Alexandre Fine Antique Maps and Books** (104 Queen East, near Jarvis, 416-364-2376), where titles on topography, travel, military history, and architecture join a specialized selection of illustrated volumes from earlier centuries.

SECRET
MEMORIALS

Devoted to preserving the memory of six million Jewish lives destroyed during World War II, the **Holocaust Memorial Centre of Toronto** (4600 Bathurst, 416-635-2883) presents a moving and informative display of photographs and artifacts. The Hall of Memories at the heart of the center, with tiles bearing the names of Holocaust victims, provides a quiet space for prayer and remembrance. The center is open weekdays until 3 p.m. (1 p.m. on Friday) and Sunday from 11 a.m. to 4:30 p.m. There is no charge for admission, but donations are welcome. Special community awareness activities take place during Holocaust Education Week in November.

SECRET
MENAGERIES

For 75 years, jungle cats and other exotic beasts paced their cages at the Riverdale Zoo, until it closed in 1974. Four years later, the park reopened as **Riverdale Farm** (201 Winchester, east of Parliament,

416-392-6794), where cows and horses do the pacing now, behind split-rail fences instead of iron bars. Closer contact with the animals is encouraged too — you can even try your hand at milking a goat. Some of the livestock on this re-creation of a small, turn-of-the-century family farm are unusual breeds, registered with the Rare Breeds Conservancy of Canada. Programs for children and adults include quilting and weaving, while workshops teach you how to make baskets, grow herbs, and use natural dyes. Set in the midst of historic Cabbagetown, the park is a great place for picnicking and general relaxation.

Many free-ranging creatures (not counting people and pets) make urban Toronto their habitat. Raptors float serenely above the Don Valley, and raccoons rummage through backyard debris and steal grapes from ripening late-summer arbors. Skunks and foxes occasionally lead their young on nighttime forays. In recent years, even coyotes have taken up residence in High Park. Spotting creatures of another sort — animals masquerading as public sculpture — can be fun, if you know where to look. In Joe Fafard's *The Pasture* (north side of Wellington, west of Bay), three life-size bronze cows lounge amiably on a bit of green space near the Toronto-Dominion Centre. A large wooden **pelican** by an unknown artist perches on a post in Harbour Square Park, at the Toronto Island ferry docks (Queen's Quay West, at the foot of Bay), while a gigantic **woodpecker** by Toronto's Fastwürms clings to a pole in the public square immediately south of the Metro Convention Centre (55 Front West). The *Bird of Spring* (northwest corner of Dundas East and Victoria) — a bronze facsimile enlarged from an original stone carving by Etungat, a Cape Dorset Inuit artist — flaps within a circle of low fountains.

Lion prides can be sighted at a variety of locations around town: Charles Duncan McKechnie's four **concrete cats** guard an Ontario

government building at the Canadian National Exhibition, while Frances Loring's limestone lion forms part of the **Lion Monument** (Sir Casimir Gzowski Park, Lakeshore Boulevard West, between Parkside and South Kingsway), erected in 1939 to commemorate a royal visit and the opening of the Queen Elizabeth Way.

In John McEwen's ***Patterns for the Tree of Life*** (Park Street, northeast of Yonge and Bloor), startling silhouettes of wolf and deer stand in a small parkette known as Asquith Green. The College Park Patio (south of College, between Yonge and Bay) is graced by **two wooden bears and an eagle**, courtesy of sculptor Thomas Penney.

By far the liveliest and most whimsical addition to Toronto's sculptural menagerie, however, is Cynthia Short's ***Remembered Sustenance*** (Wellington West, at John): a foraging band of dog-bunnies, long-eared, four-legged creatures cavorting on the south lawn of Metro Hall.

SECRET

MEXICAN

When I first spotted **Dos Amigos** (1201 Bathurst, north of Dupont, 416-534-2528), I didn't know whether it was a new arrival or if I had simply overlooked it for years on this unlikely stretch of Bathurst, a stone's throw from the TTC yard. Who would pick a dusty spot like this? And who decided to decorate the restaurant like a Mexican theme park? In the end, it doesn't matter, because co-owners Enrique Flores and Mauricio Cabrera satisfy the appetite with a tasty chicken mole, cactus salad with black beans, and other traditional dishes.

If you're hankering for a handcrafted burrito, try **Coyote Willie** (689 Queen East, at Broadview, 416-778-4578). Soft tortillas are filled with smoky-sweet baked beans, fresh vegetarian ingredients from corn to carrot shreds, or home-barbecued chicken or beef and are served with cilantro-tinted salsa.

If you're looking for Tex-Mex, heavy on the sour cream, don't bother with **El Palenque** (653 St. Clair West, 416-656-0725), where traditional northern Mexican cooking rules: chimichangas, quesadillas, pozole, chicken mole, great guacamole, and fiery hot sauce. Four varieties of superb, chili-laced ceviche are served in three-legged rock bowls. And the big backyard patio is a perfect place to consume homemade sangria or a bottle of Mexican beer.

On Monday nights, it's appetizers only at **El Sol Mexican Gallery and Café** (1448 Danforth, east of Greenwood, 416-405-8074). Appetizers and drinks, that is, including generous margaritas made with fresh lime juice. It's fiesta night, and there's a little dance floor if you feel like stamping around. Every other day of the week, owner Yolanda Paez serves standard dinner fare under the gaze of coconut masks hanging from the walls. These and other Mexican crafts can be purchased at the downstairs shop.

SECRET
MIDDLE EASTERN

If you eat at the **Jerusalem** (955 Eglinton West, at Bathurst, 416-783-6494), don't overlook the appetizers. In fact, you can readily make a meal of them: sautéed tomatoes, crisp falafel, dreamy fried eggplant, and arguably the best tabouleh in town, accompanied by warm pita and a plateful of green olives, peppers, and pink-pickled turnip. If you're still hungry enough for a main course, the sautéed liver in garlic and pepper sauce is a pleaser. Other reliable choices include lamb kebabs and sea bass (not the fat white Chilean variety but the small, black-striped type). On weekends, the Jerusalem is often packed, so make sure you reserve ahead. Be aware that they only take reservations for groups of five or more — but that's not a bad thing, since you'll want company to share the full array of appetizers.

S E C R E T
MYSTERIES

Readers of mystery, crime, and espionage tales will adore **Sleuth of Baker Street** (1600 Bayview, south of Eglinton, 416-483-3111), a specialty bookstore with 20,000 titles shelved floor to ceiling. Author signings and other in-store events add to the excitement, and the staff will happily offer informed opinions or perform searches for the serious collector.

Deerstalkers, teddy bears, and mystery games complement the more serious objects in the **Arthur Conan Doyle Collection** (fourth floor of the Metropolitan Toronto Reference Library, 789 Yonge, one block north of Bloor, 416-393-7131). Devoted to the creator of Sherlock Holmes, the collection was started in the early 1970s and maintained for the next 20 years by librarian Cameron Hollyer. It now consists of approximately 5,000 books, including rare first editions, and 5,000 other items, such as manuscripts and original drawings from magazine serializations. The Doyle room is only open Saturday, 2 p.m. to 4 p.m., or by appointment.

If you're bored with *Columbo* or *Prime Suspect* reruns and want something a little more interactive, consider dining in suspicious company at the **Mysteriously Yours Mystery Dinner Theatre** (2026 Yonge, two blocks north of Davisville, 416-486-7469). Murderous tales unfold when someone you've just met during the three-course gourmet meal meets an unfortunate demise and the house detective is called in. Be prepared to answer a few probing questions. You can also choose to skip the food and go straight to the investigation.

Toronto's longest-running theater production, Agatha Christie's *The Mousetrap*, has been baffling audiences at the **Toronto Truck Theatre** (94 Belmont, 416-922-0084) for more than 20 years. The cast has changed, but the thrill hasn't gone.

SECRET
NEW AGE

If you're seeking the center of all knowledge, you might start by visiting the **Omega Centre** (29 Yorkville, northeast of Yonge and Bloor, 416-975-9086), a bookstore and healing arts center devoted to self-discovery. Titles point toward every conceivable enlightenment path, including acupuncture, aromatherapy, karmic astrology, Rolfing, runes, and Wicca. Crystals and inspirational tapes are available, and the store calendar advertises a crowded schedule of events, from deep trance channeling to feng shui consultations.

S E C R E T
NEW SOUNDS

The **Music Gallery** (St. George the Martyr Anglican Church, 197 John, 416-204-1080, www.musicgallery.org) specializes in avant-garde performances that may or may not qualify as musical but always engage listeners' attention. From ethnocentric and electroacoustic music to experimental, free jazz, and dance/percussion collaborations, the schedule continues to be acoustically challenging. Operating since 1976, the Music Gallery hosts musicians from around the world and has produced more than 1,000 concerts, 40 albums, and 300 radio programs. Guest composers and performers also participate in a range of lecture and workshop programs for the Artists' Education Series. And the **Music Gallery Institute** (219-60 Atlantic, 416-588-2514) now offers community music education programs for kids and adults. Under the direction of composer, percussionist, and educator Barry Prophet, the institute delivers creative instruction in such areas as world percussion, multiple guitar ensemble, and computer-assisted music.

S E C R E T
NUDITY

When people shed their clothes, they tend to behave in a different manner: decidedly affable, less aggressive, and more open. Most nudists would concur — but, then, they're more prone to being agreeable, aren't they? Because public nudity is not allowed in Toronto (or Ontario at large) — although a recent reversal of the law permits women to go topless — those who like to socialize au naturel meet in private spaces, often under the auspices of a club or naturist organization.

Most naturist clubs and resorts seek seclusion in areas outside Toronto, away from the urban core. For more information, contact the **Federation of Canadian Naturists** (416-410-6833, www.fcn.ca), which sells *The Canadian Guide to Naturist Resorts and Beaches*.

Within the city limits, the Toronto chapter of the **Ontario Roaming Bares** (www.orbtoronto.com) organizes member events such as swim nights at Toronto pools, potlucks, kids' days, and bowling parties. TNT!MEN (416-925-9872, ext. 3010), or Totally Naked Toronto Men Enjoying Nudity, sponsors house parties, potluck dinners, camping trips, and other naked social events for members, as well as bar nights and picnics open to anyone. Although most of those involved are gay or bisexual, membership is open to any man. Events that allow nonmembers typically charge $5 admission. Regular rendezvous include monthly nude swim nights at the **Harrison Baths** (15 Stephanie, two blocks north of Queen, just west of McCaul). Several Toronto bars, including **Toolbox** (508 Eastern, 416-466-8616), **The Barracks** (56 Widmer, 416-593-0499), and **Spa Excess** (105 Carlton, 416-260-2363) also host regular naked nights and underwear parties, where TNT!MEN get special rates. Call the hot line for late-breaking news and announcements.

The only public place in Toronto where you can legally doff your clothes and swim naked is **Hanlan's Point Clothing Optional Beach**, located on the Toronto Islands. Popular with nude sunbathers for decades, Hanlan's Point Beach was officially designated as a nude beach from 1894 to 1930. In May 1999, the City of Toronto once again declared the southern portion of the beach clothing optional, and Toronto Parks and Recreation now provides maintenance and lifeguard service. Shower and change facilities are located nearby, next to the tennis courts, and the beach provides a good front-row seat for the annual fireworks display and the CNE air show. To get there, take the Hanlan's Point ferry from the terminal at the foot of Bay Street (for ferry schedules, call 416-392-8193, or visit www.city. toronto.on.ca/parks/to_islands/ferry.htm). On the island, the beach is about a 10-minute walk from the ferry dock. Follow the paved path away from the airport, turning right at the tennis court. You'll see a break in the trees to the west, which leads to the supervised (clothed) swimming area. Continue walking south along the beach, past the barrier screen, until you reach a fenced section with a sign identifying the area as clothing optional. For information about summer beach or winter swim night schedules, contact the **Hanlan's Beach Naturists** (416-410-6333).

Nude bathing at other Toronto beaches is illegal. However, devoted naturists have been known to discreetly risk the law at several locations. The very long beach below the **Scarborough Bluffs** (see "Secret Scarborough") may provide a measure of privacy, due to the slightly difficult access, but police boat patrols are not uncommon. Sandy, secluded **Beechgrove**, at the east end of East Point Park, also attracts a number of skinny-dippers. To get there, take Lawrence east past Morningside, turn south on Beechgrove Drive, and follow it to the small parking lot at the very end, past the treatment plant and railway tracks. A gravel road leads down to the lakeshore, and the beach area is less than 10 minutes to the east, near Highland Creek's mouth.

Surprisingly, they do sell T-shirts and a few other items of clothing at **The Nudist Store** (7581 Jane, Unit 11, Concord, 905-760-9878). Naked chefs will appreciate the nudist apron, especially when frying bacon first thing in the morning. The pillow pocket beach towel is another useful item: a large pocket with Velcro fastener is designed to hold your wallet, keys, and other valuables — hey, where else are you gonna put them? Stuff your clothes into the pocket and it doubles as a pillow. If you're heading to the beach, or even the backyard, you'll want sun care products too — remember, some parts are more sensitive than others — so take along a bottle of bronzing lotion, aloe gel, or after-sun moisturizer, all "made by nudists, for nudists." Also on sale are books and magazines extolling the virtues of the naturist lifestyle. There's a film-processing service run by the Federation of Canadian Naturists (privacy guaranteed) and a bulletin board for local event listings, including nude swim schedules. Don't be alarmed if you see a man in the store wearing only socks, shoes, and a wristwatch — owner Malcolm Scott spends his working hours in the buff. Clothing is optional for visitors, but you don't need to leave home without it, because there's a convenient change room onsite. And there's no need to worry about window shoppers — thick wooden blinds keep out curious gazers.

SECRET
OCCULT

❊

The array of oils and incense, inks and sprinkling salts, tarot cards and Celtic jewelry at the **Occult Shop** (109 Vaughan, just north of St. Clair, west of Bathurst, 416-656-6564) is spellbinding. Browse the bookshelves for the word on dreams and divinations, numerology, Norse mythology, New Age, and Wicca, while breathing in the aura

of spirituality and spice. Jars and bins of medicinal herbs, as well as
ceremonial daggers, candles, and other tools of the trade, round off
the fare here. In the upstairs space, known as GreenMan, the **Wiccan
Church of Canada** (Toronto branch) holds its Sunday-evening rituals
during cold weather, as well as Tuesday-night "craft" classes. Every
three weeks or so, the WCC also offers a Sunday-afternoon family circle, open to anyone with children. During the summer, WCC circles
are held at fire pit #4 at **Serena Gundy Park** (northwest of Leslie
and Eglinton East). Call the shop for more information.

Pagans from all traditions gather for drinks and discussion at the
Pagan Pub Moot (at the Imperial Public Library, 58 Dundas East,
416-977-4667), held on the third Monday of every month and sponsored by the Pagan Federation of Canada (call Karen at 416-635-
5981 for more information). The "library," located upstairs from the
Imperial Pub Tavern a block or so east of Yonge Street, is a laidback
watering hole with book-lined walls and jukebox jazz, popular with
students from nearby Ryerson Polytechnical University. Drop in
anytime for a "brew."

S E C R E T
OPERA

The development of Canada's first permanent opera company, which
began in 1950, can be traced through the periodicals, press clippings,
thousands of pictures, tapes, playbills, and other ephemera gathered
in the **Joan Baillie Archives of the Canadian Opera Company**
(227 Front East, 416-363-6671). The collection also includes materials

dating back as far as 1825. Set models and posters are displayed in the exhibit area, and the upstairs music library holds more than 5,000 operatic recordings, plus videotapes of Canadian Opera Company productions. Open by appointment on Monday, Wednesday, and Thursday, 9:30 a.m. to 3 p.m.

S E C R E T

ORNITHOPTER

Although Leonardo da Vinci drafted plans as early as 1490 for a human-powered version of the ornithopter — a contraption that flies by flapping its wings like a bird — no one managed to successfully build a working device until the late 20th century, when Jeremy Harris and James DeLaurier designed their modern-day, engine-powered flying machine at the University of Toronto Institute for Aerospace Studies.

Flight with mechanical flapping wings is one of humanity's oldest aeronautical dreams, and it continues to be one of our greatest challenges. Despite fantastical achievements like space travel, supersonic speeds, and around-the-world nonstop flights, engineers have been unable to accomplish this early goal.

On September 4, 1991, a remotely piloted model with a 10-foot wingspan, built by the Harris-DeLaurier team as part of **Project Ornithopter** (www.ornithopter.net), completed the first successful sustained flight. That milestone was officially recognized by the Fédération Aéronautique Internationale. A full-scale piloted aircraft has since been built. In recent tests, it self-accelerated on level ground to speeds allowing brief lift-offs. Although it had not yet, at the time of writing, achieved sustained flight, it may very well have attained that goal by the time you read this.

In any event, following its final test flight, the ornithopter will be retired and put on view at the **Toronto Aerospace Museum** (65 Carl Hall Road, south of Sheppard, west of Dufferin, 416-638-6078), where much of the testing has taken place. Only a couple of years old, the fledgling museum has already acquired a diverse collection of military, commercial, and experimental aircraft and artifacts. The all-volunteer staff devotes much of its time to various restoration projects. One project of particular note is the construction of a full-scale, museum-quality "interpretation" of the famous Avro Arrow CF-105 Mk. 1. It doesn't fly, but it looks like the real thing and is able to taxi around under its own steam.

The museum is open to the public only a few days a week (call ahead to confirm the hours), but group tours can be arranged. A gift shop onsite carries clothing, jigsaw puzzles, kites, and model aircraft. To get there, take the 108 Downsview, the 86 Sheppard West, or the 84 Sheppard West bus from Downsview subway, and ask the driver to let you off at the Downsview Park entrance. Enter the park and follow John Drury Lane to Carl Hall Road, then turn left and continue east over the railway tracks to the museum.

On the first Monday of every month from 7 p.m. to 9:30 p.m., the museum hosts meetings of the **International Plastic Modelers Society, Toronto Chapter** (Garfield Ingram, 416-239-7465, www.ipmstoronto.on.ca), a large group of model-plane-building enthusiasts who gather to exchange ideas and show off their lovingly crafted scale replicas. Monthly seminars by advanced modelers investigate the finer points of airbrushing, realistic weathering, detailing, and building from scratch. Guests are welcome, but no glue-sniffing is allowed.

The Toronto Aerospace Museum is fittingly located in one of the historic production hangars built by de Havilland Aircraft of Canada, which first set up shop here in Downsview in 1929. The manufacturing facility grew significantly during World War II. At its peak, the plant employed more than 7,000 workers and churned out as many as three planes per day. Following the war, de Havilland returned to the job of building civilian aircraft. But the Government of Canada decided this spot, with its hangars and airfield, was perfectly suited to become an air force base. The Department of National Defence expropriated hundreds of local properties, and Royal Canadian Air Force Station Downsview was established to defend Toronto industry.

Decommissioned as a military base in 1996, a portion of the site has now been designated as Canada's first national urban park, with a mixed-use mandate that includes recreational and cultural uses. **Downsview Park** (located between Keele Street and Allen Road, south of Sheppard Avenue, 416-952-2227) is a work in progress — indeed, the full development is expected to last 20 years or more. The plan for this unique green space was developed by a team of visionary architect-designers, led by Pritzker Architecture Prize winner Rem Koolhaas. A scale model of the park-to-be is on view at the park office (35 Carl Hall Road, 416-952-2222). The main entrance to the park is located at John Drury Drive and Sheppard Avenue.

Elsewhere on the Downsview site is the **Supply Depot**, a 910,000-square-foot warehouse that was originally built to withstand an atomic blast. Currently used for storage and filmmaking, this fascinating remnant of the area's former life as a military base will ultimately be redeveloped as a high-tech research center.

S E C R E T

OSTRICH

Commercial ostrich farming originated in South Africa in the mid-1800s, when the big flashy feathers were the height of fashion. Indeed, until the fashion market for ostrich plumes collapsed, feathers were the only ostrich product being produced. Nowadays, ostrich farming has spread to the United States, Canada, Mexico, and Australia but not because tall feathers are back in vogue. Ostrich leather is being turned into shoes and briefcases, feathers have found a new use in industrial cleaning applications for computer and car manufacturers, ostrich oil is suitable for skin care cosmetics, and ostrich meat — high in protein and iron, low in cholesterol and calories — is turning up on fine-dining menus. How does it taste? Unlike other exotic meats, you won't hear anyone say it tastes like chicken. Rather, most people liken it to beef or a cross between beef and duck.

Try it yourself at **Goldfish** (372 Bloor West, 416-513-0077), where grilled ostrich is served with celery root agnolotti, sugar snap peas, roasted red peppers, and wild berry sauce. This cool, contemporary restaurant in the Annex serves up other great mains, like striped bass and hazelnut-crusted rack of lamb, as well as great frites (order them on the side). Ostrich can also be found on the Asian- and Caribbean-influenced menu at **Sarkis** (67 Richmond East, at Church, 416-214-1337), where it's pan seared and served with smoked duck prosciutto. If you'd rather try your own recipe at home, you can buy vacuum-packed ostrich meat at the **Big Carrot Natural Food Market** (348 Danforth, near the Chester subway, 416-466-2129). Bon appétit!

SECRET
OXYGEN

Rather than knocking back a martini after a hard day at the office, why not unwind with a breath of fresh air at the **O2 Spa Bar** (2044 Yonge, 416-322-7733)? Twenty minutes of inhaling medical-grade oxygen can give your body's oxidation reduction system an aerobic boost. But don't think of it as a hospital procedure — the O2 Spa Bar, looking like a cross between a massage parlor and a hip neighborhood café, promotes a health-conscious lifestyle, not a medical rescue. Options include aromatherapy oxygen (a little lavender essence, or other essential oil, is added to the air); private rooms with calming, colorful fish tanks embedded in the wall; seaweed facials and various massage treatments; and a fruit and vegetable juice bar, if you really do need a drink. The juice is free when you gas up on Sunday, and every Wednesday is an all-day happy hour, when the O2 is half price.

SECRET
PADDLING

As Kenneth Grahame observed in *The Wind in the Willows*, "There is nothing — absolutely nothing — half so much worth doing as simply messing about in boats." Those who share the sentiment can learn the finer points of paddling, portaging, and even whitewater kayaking at the **Harbourfront Canoe and Kayak School** (283-A

Queen's Quay West, 416-203-2277), the bright blue-and-yellow building at the Nautical Centre. The school also arranges out-of-town adventures and rents small craft for boating around the bay or exploring the Toronto Islands archipelago. Less adventurous travelers can try their sea legs (figuratively speaking — standing up is strictly discouraged) in a canoe on the one-and-a-half-acre pond just outside the Water's Edge Café at nearby **Harbourfront Centre** (235 Queen's Quay West). The school also arranges several special events during the summer. There are Big Buffet Paddles, which include an island picnic, and team-paddling excursions in the governor's canoes — replicas from the era of the voyageur fur trade — complete with costumes and historian guide.

The **Queen's Quay Yachting Centre** (275 Queen's Quay West, 416-203-3000) rents sailboats to certified sailors approved by the Canadian Yachting Association and powerboats to any other would-be sea captain (you must sign a waiver). Fees range from $45 to $395 an hour. Lessons are also available.

The **Argonaut Rowing Club** (1225 Lakeshore Boulevard West, 416-532-2803) has been active since the 1870s, two decades before rowing became an Olympic sport in 1896. So the club is well qualified to teach boating for beginners, through eight classes held over four weekends. Although a rowing machine may work the same muscles, wrestling a 12-foot oar in unison with your boat mates is an altogether different experience.

S E C R E T
PAINTBALL

Ready to commune with your inner warrior? Then strap on a hot, sweaty face mask and protective goggles, pick up your carbon-dioxide-powered Sheridan VM 68 semiautomatic or Tippman pump-action rifle, grab a bag of ammo, and step onto the 50,000-square-foot killing field at **Sgt. Splatter's Project Paintball** (54 Wingold, just north of Eglinton and Dufferin, 416-781-0991). Oh, and don't forget to tuck in your coveralls, 'cause, damn, those little paintball suckers can hurt if they catch you in a soft spot! Sgt. Splatter's lays claim to Canada's largest indoor paintball arena. Resembling a movie set from hell, the sand-covered "City under Siege" features multiple playing levels, abandoned vehicles, dozens of shell-shocked buildings, sandbags, and special sound, light, and pyrotechnic effects. Choose from more than 20 different scenarios, including Capture the Flag, Attack and Defend, Nuclear Crisis, Drug Lords and D.O.A., Elimination, and P.O.W., all supervised by young but enthusiastic game leaders. Sessions usually run three to four hours, with most games lasting a maximum of 10 minutes. So don't worry if you're an easy target and tend to get shot a lot — you'll soon be back in the action. Invite all your friends and arch-enemies for a group event, because it's way more fun to shoot someone you know. Children under 13 aren't permitted. Serious war-game enthusiasts will insist on visiting the Pro Shop to check out the latest in electropneumatic paintball guns, barrels, motorized feeders, high-pressure air systems, sight frames, camouflage clothing, and more. If you're between flights at Pearson International with a few hours to spare, Sgt. Splatter's has a second location only five minutes from the airport (79 Bramsteele, Brampton, 905-781-0991). The playing field is smaller (3,100 square feet), but it's open 24 hours!

SECRET
PARACHUTING

If you're afraid of heights, just skip ahead to the next section of *Secret Toronto*. You don't need a bad case of vertigo to complicate an otherwise healthy fear of death as you contemplate the earth from 2,800 feet in the air, perched in the open door of a small plane. If you can muster the courage, then pack a lunch and drive north to the **Parachute School of Toronto** (Highway 10 or Highway 400 north to Highway 9, west to Highway 6, north to the second set of lights in the town of Arthur, right on Frederick to the edge of town, five kilometers [three miles] along to the second road on the right, then one kilometer [0.6 mile] along that road to the second place on the left, 1-800-361-5867, www.parachuteschool.com). It's about a two-hour drive, and registration begins at 9 a.m., so set the alarm clock. The one-day course begins with classroom instruction, followed by training drills: throwing yourself from a barn loft, walking off tall platforms, and getting intimate with the emergency chute. By late afternoon, you are (theoretically) ready to jump. After your instructor gently coaxes you out of the plane, and your parachute automatically opens via a static line, you can relax and spend the next two and a half minutes watching the earth come up to greet you.

S E C R E T

PARKS

Toronto is a city of parks, and this predilection for green space means you're never very far from a bench or a carpet of grass to relax on. Favored by local dog walkers, **Trinity Bellwoods Park** (south of Dundas West, between Crawford and Gore Vale, to Queen West) served as the set for a first film by Bruce McCullough of *Kids in the Hall* fame, appropriately titled *Dog Park*. Well treed and picturesque, the park has tennis courts, a wading pool for kids, a new community center with an indoor swimming pool, and an outdoor winter skating rink. The bold stone and ironwork gates at the southern end on Queen Street West may seem out of place, an ostentatious entrance for a mere park. But they once belonged to Trinity College, originally built on this site in the 1850s. The college was relocated in the 1920s — not moved but rebuilt in replica on Hoskins Avenue on the University of Toronto campus. The original college was demolished in 1956, leaving only the gates.

Toronto's industrial and geological heritage is preserved in tandem at the **Don Valley Brick Works** (entrance off Bayview, in the Don Valley north of Danforth, 416-392-1111), a park created on a former manufacturing site. Bricks and other clay products produced at this plant — which opened in the 1880s and remained in operation for over a hundred years — helped build Toronto, including such landmarks as Osgoode Hall, the University of Toronto's Hart House and Convocation Hall, Toronto General Hospital, and the Canadian Imperial Bank of Commerce at Broadview and Danforth, not far from the brick works. Of the 15 or 16 structures onsite, the most prominent is a kiln chimney with the word VALLEY spelled vertically in white brick, the last of four such towers that together advertised the company's presence and purpose. Toronto artist Sandy Ducros's 290-foot-long mural, painted along the south side facing Bayview, celebrates both the natural and human history of the site. Walkways and wildflower gardens encourage visitors to explore the surrounding quarry, creek, and wetlands, which are gradually being coaxed back to their natural state.

Rouge Park (416-392-8186), located on Scarborough's eastern boundary, has the distinction of being North America's largest urban park — 11,600 acres extending north from Lake Ontario to Steeles Avenue, engulfing the Metropolitan Toronto Zoo. But once you're there, you're guaranteed to forget the city exists. The Rouge River Valley is an ecological treasure, its woodlands, meadows, and marshes representing some of the last remaining wilderness in the Metro region. The Rouge Park strategy is designed to restore natural habitats, creating a refuge for endangered wildlife, including the eastern bluebird and Cooper's hawk. Although **Glen Rouge Campground** (off Kingston Road [Highway 2], east of the Sheppard-Port Union interchange, 416-392-2541) offers the usual amenities, you won't find picnic tables, washrooms, and groomed trails in the rest of Rouge Park. Visitors should first drop by the **Pearse House Conservation Centre** (1757 Meadowvale, north of Sheppard, opposite the Metro Zoo entrance). At the southern end, **Rouge Beach Park** (at the end of Lawrence East; take bus 54A from Lawrence East station) contains both wetlands (favored by migrating waterfowl) and a sandy beach (favored by people wanting to get wet). The **West Rouge Canoe Club** (416-281-8620) gives canoe and kayak paddling lessons, with an emphasis on water safety.

Simultaneously celebrating the urban and the natural, the **Village of Yorkville Park** (Cumberland and Bellair, just northwest of Bloor

and Bay) is a series of gardens laid out in rectangular strips symboliz-
ing the lot lines of row houses that once stood on the site. The park
is home to more than 90 varieties of native North American plants
and several open architectural structures, including a high-tech fountain composed of vertical wires. One part formal garden and one part
playground, the park centers on a massive, 650-tonne granite rock —
imported from Gravenhurst in the Muskokas, it was sawed into 135
pieces, carted south on 20 flatbed trailers, and reassembled like a jigsaw puzzle. Feel free to clamber up and play King of the Castle. Or,
for a bird's-eye view of the entire park, try the third-floor rear window of Chapters (110 Bloor West), where the easy chairs are lined up
for book lovers to take advantage of the natural light.

SECRET
PHO
❧

Pho Hung (350 Spadina Avenue, 416-593-4274; also 200 Bloor
West, 416-963-5080) is a popular spot to enjoy steaming bowls of
Vietnamese pho (beef-stock soup), garnished with bean sprouts, fresh
basil, and wedges of lime.

Less noticeable on a strip of Ossington Avenue devoted to car
washes, karaoke bars, late-night laundromats, and Portuguese fish
stores — but no less worthy than Pho Hung — **Golden Turtle** (150
Ossington, 416-531-1601) has been dishing out delicious Vietnamese
noodle soup for 20 years. The menu offers more than 20 varieties of
pho, an equal number of rice dishes, various vermicelli combos, and a
long list of drinks, including lychee, red bean with coconut, and the
addictive iced coffee with condensed milk.

SECRET
PHOTOGRAPHY

In 1888, the Photographic Section of the Royal Canadian Institute
(see "Secret Science") became the **Toronto Camera Club** (587
Mount Pleasant, two stoplights south of Eglinton, 416-480-0720).
The first of its kind in Canada, the club is still operating successfully
more than a century later. Club members meet regularly on Monday
nights from September to May. In addition, the club hosts social
events, workshops, and a Thursday-night lecture series (preregistra-
tion is encouraged, although tickets may also be available at the
door). Guest speakers share tips and techniques, accompanied by
stunning slide shows. Phone for the latest schedule.

Five of Toronto's most interesting photo galleries are within easy
walking distance of one another. Exhibitions at the **Jane Corkin
Gallery** (179 John, Suite 302, 416-979-1980), just north of Queen
Street, often juxtapose modern masters with historical works. An
inventory of fine art photography by Canadian and international
artists is also available for viewing and purchasing. South of Queen,
in a converted warehouse building just east of Spadina (see "Secret
Warehouses"), you'll find the nonprofit, artist-run **Gallery 44, Centre
for Contemporary Photography** (401 Richmond West, Suite 120,
416-979-3941). The exhibits here emphasize innovative approaches
to material and subject matter, often extending beyond pure photography to include video and installation elements. The center also
maintains resource material on contemporary Canadian photography,
provides production facilities for members and community groups, and
offers workshops on new and traditional photo techniques. Similarly,
Gallery TPW, Toronto Photographers Workshop (80 Spadina

Avenue, Suite 310, 416-504-4242), located a little farther south on Spadina, supports the production and exhibition of contemporary photo-based art. A highlight is TPW's annual fund-raising event in December, when hundreds of photographs go on sale at great prices. Farther west on Queen, the **Stephen Bulger Gallery** (700 Queen West, 416-504-0575) emphasizes photography that serves as social documentation, like Larry Towell's stunning work from El Salvador. On Saturday afternoons, from noon to 5 p.m., you can extend your photo binge by visiting the **Ydessa Hendeles Art Foundation** (778 King West, west of Bathurst, 416-413-9400), situated in a former uniform factory. The Hendeles gallery hosts some of Toronto's most important photo exhibits, often combining historical collections with new media pieces.

SECRET
PIZZA

Amid the crowded bustle of Kensington Market, it's easy to miss the tiny little storefront of **Pizzabilities R Endless** (69 Kensington, 416-971-5521). But if you want to experience pizza that's not common-place, don't miss this opportunity. Some people like to cut corners, as the store flyer reminds us, but the corners at Pizzabilities have literally been left in place: the pizza is cooked in big, rectangular 18- by 26-inch pans and then put on racks in the store window. The owner shuns the "gourmet" label, but the ingredients — including spinach in garlic, fresh goat cheese, eggplant, asparagus, and portobello mushrooms — say otherwise.

Thin-crust gourmet pizza is only one of the reasons — albeit a very good one — to visit **Terroni** (720 Queen West, 416-504-0320), a long and narrow sandwich bar that's always hopping with youthful energy. Maybe it's the espresso and good music, or the constantly bantering staff, but Terroni's an excellent spot to enjoy a quick lunch.

For years, University of Toronto students have been subsisting on affordable slices from **Cora Pizza** (656 1/2 Spadina Avenue, at Harbord, 416-922-1188). And students know pizza the way truck drivers know truck stops — when you see 'em lining up in front of a particular spot, you know it's worth pulling over.

Aside from pasta, kebabs, panzerotto, and salads, **Big Man's Pizza** (1528 Bayview, south of Eglinton, 416-485-8888) turns out more than 40 varieties of mouthwatering, stone-baked gourmet pizza — heaven for vegetarians and meat lovers alike.

SECRET
PLANE SPOTTING

There are no authorized viewing locations for plane spotters at **Pearson International Airport** (416-247-7678). The glass-walled departure lounges don't count, since you have to buy a ticket to get in. Besides, they don't offer good sightlines for much more than an inspection of the general condition of the plane you're about to board. Dedicated hobbyists — who consider it a vocation (if not a *va*cation) to spend hours and days in close proximity to the airport watching the big jets come and go — have a limited number of lookouts to choose from. In fact, Toronto plane spotters may be an endangered species, due to the gradual destruction of their natural habitat. Former favorite locations like Silver Dart Drive at the end of runway 24L have been restricted by barricades and plastered with "No Stopping" signs, while the panoramic view from the rooftop of the **Terminal One parking garage** at Pearson will eventually disappear when the building is demolished as part of the official Terminal Development Project. And stopping alongside Highway 427 near the airport (or anywhere else on this speed-crazy freeway) is considered reckless self-endangerment and not worth the risk.

Still, the Toronto airport is one of the most popular in Canada among aerophiles. With three terminals, four main runways, and 30 taxiways, it's Canada's biggest airport and the 25th busiest in the world, serving more than 50 airlines and close to 28 million passengers a year. Expansion will eventually raise Pearson's annual capacity to 50 million. (For more information about the airport, including plans for the future, visit the **Greater Toronto Airport Authority** [GTAA] Web site at www.lbpia.toronto.on.ca.)

Some watchers recommend the parking lot of the **Boeing Canada** plant on Airport Road (go north past all the airport entrances, past the hangars, and watch for the gates on your left), where you can walk right up to the fence line, close enough to feel the engine blast during takeoffs. This front-row seat is located on private property, however, and it's only suitable on weekends, when the plant is closed.

A safer bet is right across the street, in the picnic area beside **Wendy's** (6585 Airport, 905-678-7846). The view of the runway is obstructed by an auto body shop, but the picnic tables are positioned directly under the approach path for runway 24R — you can almost grab the landing gear as the planes roar overhead. There's a bit of a back draft, so make sure you hold onto your fries when the big ones go by. If you plan to stay for awhile, bring a blanket and flop out on the grass. It's a great spot for families with kids or a fun date.

Serious spotters come equipped with scanners to monitor airline frequencies and eavesdrop on conversations between pilots and air traffic controllers. For a crash course in technical matters of air traffic control, including an introduction to the phonetic alphabet, aircraft call signs, and runway numbering, visit aviation buff Peter Ivakitsch's **Canadian Aeronautical Communications Web site** (www.canairradio.com). You'll also find updates about the ongoing petition to the GTAA to create an official Pearson observation area. While you're browsing the Web, why not listen to a live air traffic control feed of Toronto arrivals at **Squawkident.com** (www.squawkident.com/livefeed. html)?

If you share Mr. Ivakitsch's passion for planes, you may want to pick up your very own scanner at **Aviation World** (195 Carlingview, 416-674-5959), conveniently located near the airport, a block south of the Dixon Road hotel strip. Owner and former 747 pilot Len Neath began selling books and collectibles from his basement in 1967 but soon ran out of room. Now stocked with thousands of books, plastic model kits and hobby supplies, electronics, travel accessories, and pilot gear, this store is a paradise for the true aviation enthusiast. You can pick up a pair of Randolph aviator sunglasses (standard issue for US military pilots) or a chronograph watch with more dials than you'll know what to do with. It's open seven days a week, and the parking lot it shares with the punningly named Landing Strip nude dance bar next door is, not coincidentally, a pretty good spot to watch the airplanes strut their stuff in the skies overhead.

Wherever you choose to sit and watch, you'll fit right in with the regulars if you take a lunch and make a day of it. But please, don't feed the seagulls! Feeding attracts a crowd, and birds around the airport can spell trouble for the planes. Bird strikes are a serious threat to safety, and the GTAA will do whatever it can to dissuade the presence of feathery flocks — including trying to keep plane spotters at bay. The situation is so serious, in fact, that the airport has hired mercenaries to help manage the problem — predatory peregrine falcons, which occupy a custom-built home on top of the GTAA Administration Building and help deter other birds from lingering in the flight path.

SECRET
POETRY

The only street in Canada — and perhaps North America — named after an experimental poet is **bpNichol Lane**, running north of Sussex Avenue, between Huron Street and St. George Street, in the heart of the University of Toronto's student housing district. Governor General's Award winner bpNichol, known and loved for his visual (or "concrete") poetry, died in 1988, and in 1994 this alley behind the historic literary press **Coach House** (401 Huron, rear, 416-979-7989) was given his name. One of Nichol's poems, drilled into the *concrete* road, was unveiled at the renaming ceremony. A broadly grinning, life-size cardboard cutout of bpNichol peers out at the lane from inside Coach House. If it's not a busy day, someone at the press might be willing to show poetry fans around the collection of vintage printing press equipment inside the shop. The door is on the opposite side of the building from bpNichol Lane.

SECRET
POLITICS

If CPAC, the parliamentary channel, isn't riveting or real enough, you can witness the government at work firsthand from the gallery at **Queen's Park** (1 Queen's Park, College and University, 416-325-7500). The provincial legislature assembles from March to June and September to December. Get passes for the fourth-floor public gallery from the information desk at the entrance. The hulking, Romanesque parliament building itself is worth visiting for its architectural interest as well as the historical portraits and changing exhibits throughout the main-floor hallways that promote Ontario's history, culture, and heritage. Built in the late 1880s on the former site of King's College — the first University of Toronto building, which also served briefly as a lunatic asylum before making way for the politicians — Queen's Park up close reveals a treasure of carved detail and interior decoration. Free tours of the building run almost hourly in the summer and less frequently during the rest of the year.

The **Legislative Dining Room**, facing the foot of the stairs in the basement of Queen's Park, serves wonderful — and inexpensive — lunch specials. White tablecloths, subdued conversation, and the absence of background music contribute to the peaceful atmosphere. The restaurant is only open on weekdays from 11:30 a.m. to 2:30 p.m. Reservations can be made but aren't required. (There's also a nearby cafeteria, open throughout the day.)

Municipal politics are played out in one of Toronto's most recognizable structures, the neo-Expressionist **New City Hall** (100 Queen West, at Bay, 416-338-0338). The showy monument by Finnish archi-

tect Viljo Revell — chosen by international competition in the early 1960s from submissions by 520 architects from 44 countries — consists of two curved towers cupping a flying-saucer-shaped council chamber, sitting atop a two-story podium. Pick up a brochure at the information desk in the foyer and take a self-guided tour any weekday. (The information center on the lower level is a good place to pick up maps and other material about city attractions.) **Nathan Phillips Square**, the nine-acre concrete plaza in front of City Hall, is a hub of civic activity. You can enjoy musical performances, Wednesday farmers' markets from Victoria Day through Thanksgiving, Bunnymania on Easter weekend, the huge annual **Toronto Outdoor Art Exhibition** (416-408-2754) on the second weekend in July, and a full lineup of other activities.

Serious civic debate is conducted under the auspices of the **St. Lawrence Centre Forum** (St. Lawrence Centre for the Arts, 27 Front East, 416-366-1656, ext. 271), a discussion series that brings the public together with policymakers, political commentators, and grassroots organizations for panel discussions and presentations about current issues in the city. A prominent feature of these evening events, and often the liveliest part, is the segment set aside for questions from the audience. The forum has been going strong since 1970, when it was sparked by public opposition to plans for the Spadina Expressway — an ill-conceived project that was subsequently halted in its tracks. Forum organizers recently launched a new initiative, Forum on Wheels, that takes the discussion to other community gathering spots around town.

S E C R E T
POOL
❧

Fifteen antique pool tables, a martini bar, and stylishly comfortable decor, including Persian rugs and cushy sofas, set the tone at the **Academy of Spherical Arts** (38 Hanna, 416-532-2782). Tucked away in the old industrial warehouse district (just off Atlantic Avenue, south of King Street), the academy sports a casual, club-like atmosphere, where patrons are more likely to be sipping Scotch than swilling beer. Arts of the nonspherical variety, from the academy's permanent collection as well as traveling exhibits, are displayed in the John Brunswick and Samuel May galleries. You can shoot stick on more old tables with character upstairs at the **Rivoli Pool Hall** (334 Queen West, 416-596-1501), above the fashionable restaurant and bar of the same name.

Crave a late-night game? You can rack 'em up into the wee hours at **Central Billiards** (468 Queen West, at Augusta, 416-504-9494). The 24-hour establishment is open to members only (an affordable $10 a year) — but you can get a temporary membership at the door for two loons. The club is licensed and has 20 tables to choose from. And out east on the Danforth, in the land of souvlaki, patrons of the **Billiards Academy** (485 Danforth, upstairs, 416-466-9696) keep the balls rolling 24 hours a day. This smoky, no-frills establishment epitomizes the term "pool hall."

Hidden away on a small downtown street, the **Charlotte Room** (19 Charlotte, 416-598-2882) was voted one of the top 10 billiard rooms in the world by *Billiards Digest US* in 1998. This comfortable club offers decent food and a fully stocked bar, live musical entertainment, and special events, including snooker tournaments, wine tastings, and theme parties like Hawaiian Night or Halloween. There's even an occasional karaoke night. Not your usual pool hall.

SECRET
PRIX FIXE

During the day, **Smalltalk Bakery and Restaurant** (1580 Bayview, 416-483-8400) is a casual spot for sandwiches, wild mushroom omelettes, fresh croissants, and other lunch or brunch-type fare. A few items on the daytime menu, though — like the mussels in lemongrass, curry, and coconut milk sauce or the watercress salad with mango and black walnuts — hint at the elegant, upscale flavors that appear when the white tablecloths come out for dinner. Six days a week, at 6 p.m., the menu converts to a prix-fixe affair. Chef Ros McCurdy creates everything from scratch and likes to shuffle the choices from month to month (fish dishes are a favorite). No matter what the selection, $35 gets you an appetizer, an entrée, and a delicious dessert. You can request a few extras (for a few extra bucks), but there's no ordering à la carte.

SECRET
PSYCHIATRY

Not many people would go out of their way to enter an asylum, but the **Queen Street Mental Health Centre** (1001 Queen West, 416-

535-8501), with its glass-fronted entrance hall stretching toward the sidewalk on Queen, seems to invite passersby to step inside. In 1989, someone took the invitation too far by driving a stolen car at high speed straight down Ossington Avenue, bumping over the sidewalk, smashing through the front doors, and carrying on merrily down the corridor a full 100 yards. A row of concrete planters along the street now prevents unauthorized vehicular traffic, but pedestrians are still welcome. Anyone with an interest in mental health will find it rewarding to visit the **Archives on the History of Canadian Psychiatry and Mental Health** (416-535-8501, ext. 2159). Early-20th-century case files from the Toronto General Nervous Ward, biographies, artworks relating to mental illness, and reams of research papers and publications are housed at the archives, which are open by appointment on Tuesday and Thursday. Currently in storage awaiting permanent display space are the records and artifacts collected by the **Museum of Mental Health Services Toronto**, including drawings of arcane medical instruments and a trepanned human skull from the 1600s (when the treatment for releasing evil spirits involved the boring of circular holes with a trephine).

The Mental Health Centre is also home to the innovative **Workman Theatre Project** (416-583-4339), a nonprofit theater company where people receiving mental health services work hand in hand with the professional theater community to create public performances. Every year, one main-stage piece is mounted at the 300-seat Joseph Workman Auditorium (1001 Queen West), while shorter works play at other venues around town. In mid-November, the weeklong **Rendezvous with Madness Film Festival** (www.rendezvous withmadness.com) explores the facts and mythologies of mental illness. Screenings of short and feature-length films are combined with postscreening panel discussions, designed to promote a better understanding of mental health and related issues.

SECRET
PUBLIC ART

If you find yourself near a streetcar stop on the Spadina Avenue LRT route, anywhere between Bloor and Richmond, and there's a big pole at the stop, take a minute to look up — way up. Perched well above normal sight lines, several sculptures mark historically significant districts along Spadina. Commissioned as part of a "grand avenue" refurbishing project when the transit line was installed, the **Spadina LRT Public Art** also includes more easily visible installations, such as Stephen Cruise's monument to the fashion district: a nine-foot-high stack of colored buttons capped by a bronze thimble. This display, at the Richmond and Spadina intersection, is completed by several trees and two little buttons that function as seats, meant to encourage "short-term usage" of the site. At the north end of the line, Susan Schelle and Mark Gomes have created a playful parkette on Bloor Street, including a checkerboard plaza and several stainless-steel leaf cutouts representing the long-gone Carolinian forest. Small plaques identify each work on the Spadina LRT line, but you may have to cross over to the streetcar platform on the median strip to find them.

SECRET
RAVES

Toronto's musical underground takes the form of raves — all-night dance parties that happen randomly at no fixed address. If you feel like working up a thirst, watch for rave posters affixed to telephone poles around town or tacked up in record shops. A good place to start is **Eastern Bloc Records** (336 Yonge, second floor, above Sunrise Records, 416-593-4355), purveyors of fine dance music, with in-house DJs, listening booths, and a room "totally dedicated to Jungle, Drum 'n' bass, and Happy Hardcore." Tickets to local raves can be purchased ahead of time. Other outlets include **Play de Record** (357-A Yonge, 416-586-0380) and **The Pit** (439 Yonge, 416-979-9415).

S E C R E T

READINGS

Insomniac Press publisher Mike O'Connor produces the monthly *Word: Toronto's Literary Calendar*, an essential source of literary listings — from performances and book launches to benefits, poetry slams, and schmoozefests. Find *Word* at any bookstore worth its salt, or visit the online version (www.insomniacpress.com/word).

The **Idler Pub Reading Series** (Idler Pub, 255 Davenport, 416-962-0195) packs in the literary crowd every Sunday evening. This relaxed, though often boisterous, event puts first-time readers alongside writers of renown. And if you want to make a dinner of it, the pub complements its array of beers on tap with a decent range of pastas, salads, and stir-fries.

The **U of T Bookstore Series** (416-978-7989, www.uoftbookstore.com) succeeds in mounting a serious challenge to the juggernaut **Harbourfront Reading Series** (416-973-4000, www.readings.org). A diverse array of consistently interesting readers, often paired on a common theme, takes to the podium in an equally diverse scattering of venues, from U of T's grandly orotund Convocation Hall to local brew pubs to groovy little lounges on College Street. Many of the readings are free, while tickets for paid events can be purchased ahead of time at the **University of Toronto Bookstore** (214 College, at St. George, 416-978-7900), which also stocks much more than student textbooks. The bookstore occupies the southernmost portion of the Koffler Student Services Centre — originally the City of Toronto Public Reference Library — a grand Second Classical Revival structure built in 1906 with money donated by American industrialist and philanthropist Andrew Carnegie. Inside, light from the high graceful windows illuminates both the bookshelves below and the arched ornamental ceiling above.

SECRET
ROTI

More than a decade after starting out as a little hole-in-the-wall spot with barely enough room for customers to stand inside the door, **Bacchus Roti Shop** (1376 Queen West, between Lansdowne and Dufferin, 416-532-8191) finally has a location with space for a few tables and chairs. The menu, featuring Guyanese home-style cuisine, is a little bigger too, but the shop still makes the best damn roti in Toronto. The spinach and squash combinations are amazing — with or without curried shrimp, chicken, goat, and other fixings. And the many vegetarian choices, including okra, eggplant, and mushroom, offer a nice alternative to the standard roti fillings of chickpea and potato found elsewhere.

S E C R E T

SAFE DINING

In January 2001, the City of Toronto decided to get tough on restaurants by publicly disclosing inspection results. All eating establishments must meet minimum standards for food temperatures, food handling, sanitation, dishwashing, and personal hygiene. Following a formal inspection, restaurants are required under the **Toronto Public Health Food Premises Inspection and Disclosure System** to post a color-coded food safety notice in a conspicuous spot near the entrance. The bottom line is, if you don't see green (a Pass rating), don't go in. A yellow notice means a Conditional Pass, indicating that one or more significant infractions occurred — look closely for a checklist revealing where the kitchen came up short, and either proceed with caution or come back in a few days. Red means the restaurant was deemed a serious health hazard and has been closed. Results are also posted online at **DineSafe** (www.city.toronto.on.ca/fooddisclosure/index.htm), where you can search for restaurants by name or by neighborhood. If you have questions about a particular restaurant, call **Toronto Public Health** (416-338-3663).

S E C R E T

SALVATION

When the ocean liner *Empress of Ireland* sank in the St. Lawrence River in 1914, the death toll was even greater than that of *Titanic*.

Among those who perished were 160 members of the Canadian branch of the Salvation Army, en route to a World Congress in London. The disaster profoundly shook Canadian society, and a memorial to the victims has since been erected in Mount Pleasant Cemetery (see "Secret Cemeteries"). Another tribute, accompanied by photos and documentation, forms part of the permanent display at the **Heritage Centre of the Salvation Army** (2130 Bayview, south of Lawrence East, across from the Sunnybrook Health Science Centre, 416-481-4441). Founded in 1865 by social reformer William Booth, in response to abject social and working conditions in Victorian England, the Salvation Army officially arrived in Canada with George Scott Railton in 1882. The center's display and archives illuminate the history of the Christian organization, including the evolution of the army uniform and the use of music, and its continuing philanthropic endeavors. Upstairs, the **George Scott Railton Library** (416-481-6131), maintained as part of the training academy, is also open for public study. The library and center are open weekdays from 8 a.m. to 4 p.m., although requests to visit the archives should be made in advance.

SECRET
SCARBOROUGH

The **Scarborough Bluffs**, rising more than 200 feet from Lake Ontario, are Canada's gray answer to the white cliffs of Dover. This spectacular natural formation, extending for 14.5 kilometers (nine miles) along the lakeshore, was scraped up by the Wisconsin Glacier 12,000 years ago, then slowly sculpted by waves, wind, and rain.

Views from above are best at **Scarborough Bluffs Park**, while views from below — other than by boat — are best at **Bluffer's Park**. The bluffs are highest just to the east, at the appropriately named **Cathedral Bluffs Park**. From the Victoria Park subway, take the Kingston Road 12 bus (*not* the 12A, 12B, or 12C, or you'll have a longer walk) to the intersection of Brimley Road and Barkdene Hills, then walk south on Brimley. It's a 10- or 15-minute walk to the park entrance.

S E C R E T

SCIENCE

Free science lectures on Sunday afternoons are presented every fall and winter — as they have been for more than 150 years — by the **Royal Canadian Institute** (J.J.R. MacLeod Auditorium, Medical Sciences Building, 1 King's College Circle, University of Toronto, 416-977-2983). The RCI was founded in Toronto in 1849 by a small group of civil engineers, architects, and surveyors led by Sandford Fleming (who planned Canada's transcontinental railway and created standard time). It is the oldest surviving scientific society in Canada.

S E C R E T

SCULPTURE

The **Sculptors' Society of Canada** (First Canadian Place Exchange Tower, 130 King West, at York, 416-214-0389), founded in 1928, is the only Canadian association devoted solely to the art of sculpture. The gallery displays work from the permanent collection, as well as temporary exhibitions by local and international figures.

Twice a year, a new and intriguing installation appears in the **Toronto Sculpture Garden** (115 King East, 416-485-9658), a small outdoor enclave nestled in the gap between two downtown buildings. Open from 8 a.m. until dusk, this outdoor exhibition area serves as a testing ground for artists to experiment with public space and to address issues of urban scale, materials, and context. Although the park is owned by the City of Toronto, the garden is a unique public-private collaboration, where the programming is supported by a nonprofit foundation funded by the Louis L. Odette Family.

S E C R E T
SECONDHAND BOOKS

Harbord Street between Spadina and Bathurst, hard by the University of Toronto, used to be book alley, but only a few survivors remain. **Atticus Books** (84 Harbord, 416-922-6045) is best for scholarly works in all academic disciplines, while a more general selection (with concentrations in history, literature, and science) is available at **About Books** (83 Harbord, 416-975-2668).

Elsewhere, **Eliot's Bookshop** (584 Yonge, north of Wellesley, 416-925-0268) has three floors of books, crammed floor to ceiling, and a great selection of current fiction and nonfiction. Specializing in first editions, particularly in literature and travel, **David Mason Books** (342 Queen West, second floor, east of Spadina, 416-598-1015) epitomizes the classic antiquarian bookshop. Close quarters, glass cases, lazily spinning ceiling fans, and creaky wooden floors all add to the aura, while the well-informed staff offers invaluable assistance. At **Balfour Books** (601 College, at Clinton, 416-531-9911), open seven days a week from noon till 10 p.m., the family dog keeps you company as you browse the well-stocked stacks for used and rare titles.

You might mistake the stock for new at **Annex Books** (1083 Bathurst, south of Dupont, 416-537-1852), since so many of the titles are in such great shape. But the owner's source of supply is the community of local writers and book reviewers who pass along review copies, as well as regular customers who buy new books at a pace that often outstrips the available space on their home bookshelves and need to trade them in. Annex is a particularly good spot to find Canadian literature and signed first editions, as well as small press fare.

S E C R E T

SEX SHOPS

All sizes and all colors for all tastes (including raspberry) can be found at the **Condom Shack** (231 Queen West, at the Osgoode subway, 416-596-7515, also 729 Yonge, 416-966-4226), a boisterous little boutique with a specialized stock. The lavish selection of latex is complemented by books and body lotions, clothing, cards, and games to play. Best of all, the Condom Shack stays open late — 11 p.m. during the week and midnight on Saturday — for last-minute shopping.

Safe and slippery stuff is the stock in trade of **Come As You Are** (701 Queen West, just west of Bathurst, 416-504-7934), a cooperatively owned sex-toy shop and bookstore. This "disability-positive" shop offers monthly workshops on such topics as female ejaculation and men's self-pleasuring.

When **Lovecraft** (27 Yorkville, 416-923-7331) first opened for business more than 25 years ago (originally at another location on the same street), the Yorkville area was just emerging from its hippie-era free-love phase. The coffeehouses, head shops, and Indian clothing stores were being supplanted by upscale boutiques catering to the tourist trade, the perfect market for Lovecraft's lacy lingerie and adult toys. Though it feels somewhat like a souvenir shop, the store is still fun to visit if you're prowling around today's Jaguar-infested Yorkville.

Cozy little **Good for Her** (175 Harbord, east of Bathurst, 416-588-0900) celebrates women's sexuality with a stupendous selection of high-quality vibrators and dildos, massage oils, and menstrual products, as well as books and displays of erotic work by local artists. The store provides a comfortable atmosphere for female patrons and has even introduced women-only shopping hours on Thursday (11 a.m. to 2 p.m.) and Sunday (noon to 5 p.m.); buyers and browsers of all genders and persuasions are welcome at other times. Good for Her also runs seminars on topics that range from belly dancing to tantra for beginners.

Priape (465 Church, 416-586-9914) started in Montreal in 1974 and now has a second shop in Toronto, with lots of queer stuff for sale: T-shirts, lingerie, steamy videos (from *Gangsters at Large* to *Carnaval in Rio*), calendars, CD-ROMs, and plenty of toys (including Billy dolls for boys who like leather). They also stock designer jeans and other fashionable attire.

S E C R E T
SHOES

Architect Raymond Moriyama cobbled together the vaguely shoe-shaped box that permanently houses the **Bata Shoe Museum** (327 Bloor West, at St. George, 416-979-7799), a playful, three-story secular altar to St. Crispin (the shoemaking martyr). The building has been shoehorned into a small corner plot, within walking distance of the Royal Ontario Museum and other attractions. The roof rests like a lid loosely placed on an open container, while the two street-side walls are canted inward at sidewalk level and clad with finely textured limestone that resembles raw leather. The museum's fascinating collection of more than 10,000 shoes and related artifacts is presented through interactive displays, in both permanent and temporary exhibitions, along with a program of lectures and hands-on workshops. Where else can you see French chestnut-crushing boots, human hair slippers for Australian Aboriginal executioners, and a well-preserved velvet-covered platform mule from 16th-century Venice, not to mention celebrity footwear (including Pierre Trudeau's hiking sandals, Elvis Presley's blue-and-white patent-leather loafers, and Pablo Picasso's imitation zebra-skin boots)? Don't miss the gift shop if you need sneaker-shaped key chains or shoe-motif wrapping paper.

S E C R E T
SKATING

Skaters can take to the ice at 26 different locations convenient to downtown Toronto and even more beyond. Brochures containing a map and detailed schedules are available at community information centers and elsewhere, or call the **Toronto Parks and Recreation Info Line** (416-392-1111). Most rinks open in late November, but pleasure skaters can get an early start at **Nathan Phillips Square** (100 Queen West, in front of City Hall), which opens a few weeks earlier. Special events at the Nathan Phillips rink include a New Year's Eve skating party (one of many **First Night Toronto** festivities, 416-362-3692). This is also one of the few city rinks where hockey is not permitted. Another is the kidney-shaped rink at **Harbourfront Centre** (Queen's Quay West, 416-973-4866). It's Canada's largest outdoor, artificially refrigerated ice rink, and it's open daily from 10 a.m. to 10 p.m. during the cold-weather months. There's a heated change room and skate rental and sharpening facilities, and the rink looks out over the bay toward the Toronto Islands. This is the best pleasure-skating rink in town.

Half of the Toronto rink locations have twin surfaces, so that pleasure skaters don't need shin pads to coexist with hockey players. Among these, **High Park** (Colborne Lodge Drive, south of Bloor) has pleasure skating all week on one of its rinks and commandeers both surfaces on Sunday.

For those who feel a little shaky at the ankles, the city offers a full range of skating lessons. For details, pick up a free copy of the *Toronto FUN Guide*, available at libraries and civic information centers. Basics of figure skating for those 10 years and up are taught at **Kew Gardens** (foot of Lee, off Queen Street East in the Beaches) on Thursday afternoons, followed by children's learn-to-skate classes. If you own a pair of extra-long blades, you can practice your speed skating at **Ramsden** (Yonge Street, opposite the Rosedale subway) on Saturday evenings. Families with young children, as well as adult beginners, will appreciate the various "Gentle Skate" or "Parent and Tot" hours at **Withrow Park** (Carlaw, south of Danforth). In the heart of downtown, the small, circular rink at **Ryerson** (Dundas East, at Victoria) has a few big rock sculptures to navigate around.

True Toronto cyclists know it's never too cold to ride a bike, but if you're looking for an alternative activity, the **Toronto Bicycling Network** (416-760-4191) organizes ice skating on Wednesday evenings from November to March. If you insist, you can ride your bike to the rink — just don't do it with skates on, and no bikes on the ice, please.

SECRET SKIING

If you insist on skiing only the best Ontario hills, including Horseshoe Valley and Blue Mountain, then you face at least an hour or two of driving each way. Why not do a little downhill skiing inside city limits? Snow-making machines keep the slopes covered at the **North York Ski Centre** (4169 Bathurst, at Sheppard, 416-395-7931, call 395-7934 for snow conditions), even when the rest of the city is bare. Same story at **Centennial Ski Hill** in Etobicoke (416-394-8754, call

394-5999 for snow conditions). The slopes aren't as long or steep as elsewhere, but you're guaranteed more time to enjoy the skiing and less time behind the wheel. Both resorts are open late for illuminated nighttime skiing.

SECRET
SMALL PRESS

If you're tired of the literary fare offered by mainstream book publishers, you'll want to explore the lively **Toronto Small Press Fair** (416-537-7290), a twice-yearly festival of micropresses and underground book and magazine publishers at the **Trinity-St. Paul's Centre** (427 Bloor West, just west of Spadina). Most of the items sold here — from handmade poetry pamphlets, short-story postcards, and rubber-stamped leaflets to silk-screened posters, mimeographed novels, and haiku on rye — have been published in limited editions and aren't available in any bookstore. The fair has also featured printing demonstrations, instant anthologies, panel discussions, and public readings. Look for the event in April and November, and don't be surprised if you feel inspired to start up a publishing house on your own kitchen table.

Bigger "small press" publishers, including American houses Black Sparrow, Grove Press, and Marginal (publisher of some very cool fringe books, as the name suggests), are well represented in a special section at **Pages Books and Magazines** (256 Queen West, 416-598-1447). This bookstore is one of Toronto's best, particularly when it comes to stocking unusual cultural and countercultural titles. The "body" section is popular for its range of books and magazines on bondage and discipline, tattoos, and off-the-wall art, while other areas of the store highlight drugs, cultural theory, women's studies, photography, and design.

SMALL WORLDS

Gardener Len Cullen's dream of a lifetime finally came true in 1983 when he opened **Cullen Gardens and Miniature Village** (300 Taunton West, Whitby, 905-686-1600). He transformed 30 acres of field and forest into a floral landscape, populated by 160 miniature buildings, a water slide, a kissing bridge, sprinkle ponds, and an animated historical museum. Weird but true.

SMOKE FREE

Rare in a city where strict (some might say Draconian) antismoking laws are pushing some restaurants to declare themselves bars, just so they can sidestep the rules and let their customers light up, **Smokeless Joe** (125 John, 416-591-2221) has always been a no-cigarette zone. The name of this small and quirky pub is meant to be taken literally. The joint consists of two long bars running the length of a narrow basement and an overwhelming array of bottled beers — some 250 at last count. There's also a small, ever-changing selection of microbrews on tap. To help ease your decision-making process, you're presented on arrival with several samples of whatever's currently on tap. It's a nice touch.

S E C R E T

SOOTHSAYERS

If you can handle this much spiritual energy all in one place, visit the **ESP Psychic Expo** (416-461-5306), a three-day paranormal extravaganza that usually arrives in February and again in October (either downtown at Exhibition Place or out near the airport at the International Centre). Crystal seers, astrologers, palm and tarot readers, New Age mystics, numerologists, and holistic health practitioners gather to display their wares and demonstrate their prescient powers.

S E C R E T

SPAS

Slip into a white dressing gown and submit to the soothing application of creams and buffers at the posh **Estée Lauder Spa** (50 Bloor West, 416-960-2909), tucked away on the second floor of Holt Renfrew. Or perhaps you'd prefer to lean back on the pillowed leather benches, dip your toes in the porcelain sink, and suffer a pedicure. Ah, therapy at its best — and not just for women. The four-hour package for men includes a facial, back treatment, Swedish massage, and manicure, plus lunch (served in a little room right inside the spa). Reservations are usually required three weeks ahead, but if you call on the day, you might find an opening.

The **Elmwood Spa** (18 Elm Street, 416-977-6751), set inside an 1890s building that was originally a YMCA, offers diverse beauty treatments for all body parts, from facials to foot massage, massage therapy, and water treatments in the whirlpool, sauna, and swimming pool. And, yes, men too can enjoy a little pampering. Food service is offered on the pool deck seven days a week, from 11:30 a.m. The changing menu includes such items as lemon shrimp soup and Thai spring rolls.

S E C R E T
SPORTS

Famous faces and athletic feats in Canadian sports are memorialized in **Canada's Sports Hall of Fame** (Exhibition Place, 416-260-6789). This three-story repository for trophies, uniforms, photographs, and film footage is open all year round (Monday to Friday, 10 a.m. to 4:30 p.m.), and admission is free. Established in 1955 — a year after 16-year-old Toronto swimmer Marilyn Bell galvanized the country with her 51.5-kilometer (32-mile) marathon crossing of Lake Ontario — the recently renovated venue offers three exhibit galleries with interactive kiosks, a library and archives, and a theater showing films such as *The Terry Fox Story* and *Great Moments in Canadian Sport.*

SECRET
SQUARE DANCING

American modern-style square dancing began to inch its way north into Canada by the early 1950s, and although it has become quite popular, not everyone was happy to see it arrive. The **Canadian Olde Tyme Square Dance Callers Association** (sca.uwaterloo.ca/cotsdca) was formed in 1954 with the express intention of preserving and promoting old-time Canadian dancing (predominantly influenced by English, Irish, and Scottish traditions), including favorites like "Dip and Dive," "Darlin' Nellie Grey," and "Red River Valley." Twice a year, in April and November, the association holds a big dance, featuring a four-piece band and a string of callers (the venue varies). During the regular season from September to June, dances are scheduled for the third Saturday of the month at the Buttonville Community Hall (8931 Woodbine, one kilometer [half a mile] north of Highway 7, Markham, 905-655-4719) and other Saturday evenings at a variety of Toronto venues. Refreshments are potluck (the ladies are encouraged to bring a plate of sandwiches or sweets), adult admission is $6 (kids under 10 get in free), and the doors open at 8 p.m. No partner is needed, and the callers are patient with newcomers — they'll walk you through the steps first, if required.

Many of the basic moves in old-time square dancing are similar to those in contra dancing, and the two styles share elements of historical preservation and pure enjoyment. Contra dancers form sets of two parallel lines along the length of the hall, and progressive dance sequences move each couple one position up the line. As the sequences are repeated, each couple dances with every other couple in the set. The **Toronto Country Dancers** (St. George the Martyr Anglican

Church, 205 John, north of Queen West, 905-456-1532) meet from 8:30 p.m. to 11:30 p.m. on the second, fourth, and fifth Saturday of the month, from September through June. The atmosphere is relaxed and family oriented, and the music draws on traditional Scots-Irish jigs, reels, and hornpipes, from both sides of the Atlantic. Casual clothes and soft-soled shoes are recommended. You don't need to worry if you've never danced before — the movements are much like walking to the music, and the caller teaches each dance beforehand. Arriving without a partner is perfectly okay too, since the tradition is to change partners for each dance.

SECRET
STAMPS

While many dealers confine their trade to the stamp-filled cases they shuffle from show to show, Brian Draves has taken the risk of opening a storefront business. **Sunnyside Stamps and Collectibles** (1598 King West, at Roncesvalles, 416-538-4443) is part of the notley Parkdale association known as the Sunnyside Antique Community (see "Secret Antiques"). But this shop is isolated from all the others, located around the corner in a pink-washed, angular little building overlooking Lake Ontario and busy Lakeshore Boulevard. The windows are plastered with photocopies of local postcards and postal covers, enticing passersby into the shop. Inside, the amiable Draves displays his collection of cards and stamps, including many of local origin. It's fun to poke through boxes of postcards showing Toronto as it used to be: the Riverdale Zoo when it still had tiger cages, idyllic Rosedale, and nearby Sunnyside amusement park in its golden era.

A letter mailed today from **Toronto's First Post Office** (260 Adelaide East, 416-865-1833) will bear the distinctive cancelation "York-Toronto 1833" or, by request, a replica of the original 1834 cancelation. No wonder Canada Post has acquired a reputation (certainly undeserved) for being slow to deliver the mail — 167 years is tardy by anyone's standards! Originally the fourth post office in the Town of York when postmaster James Scott Howard opened it in 1833, it officially became Toronto's first when the city incorporated in 1834. Between 1839 and 1983, the building served as a Catholic boys' school, a butter factory, and a World War I recruitment center for the Royal Air Force, among other uses. Restored by the Town of York Historical Society, Toronto's First Post Office is once again a functioning postal outlet, as well as a museum with historical exhibits, a small reference library, a gift shop with 19th-century writing materials, and a fascinating scale model of 1837 Toronto. The museum is open seven days a week, tours are available, and visitors are encouraged to try their hand at writing with a quill pen (not as easy as it sounds — be prepared to see your lovely handwriting transformed into a web of ink blobs and faint, dry scratches).

The stately stone edifice of **Postal Station K** (2384 Yonge, north of Eglinton, 416-483-7122) stands on the site formerly occupied by Montgomery's Tavern. That was the rallying spot for William Lyon Mackenzie's ragtag group of rebels, who proceeded to march south on Yonge Street during the 1837 Upper Canada Rebellion until they were dispersed by troops from Fort York (see "Secret History"). The main doorway of the post office is flanked by two stone carvings atop fluted columns — a lion and a unicorn, regal motifs repeated in the iron railing just over the doorframe. But the most interesting feature may be the royal crest on the wall above. It bears the insignia of King Edward VIII, the only one of its kind in Toronto — and no wonder, since Edward stepped down from the throne to marry Wallace Simpson in 1936, less than a year after his coronation. Not only did he shock the general public, but also his short reign gave stone carvers little time to grace buildings with his insignia.

S E C R E T

STUDIO TAPINGS

The **Canadian Broadcasting Centre** (250 Front West, 416-205-3700) hosts tapings of several TV shows in front of live audiences. Unfortunately, the CBC doesn't have a central phone number for reservations — you have to book through individual departments for tickets to popular programs like *The Red Green Show* (905-631-7450). You can track down numbers by navigating the labyrinthine CBC Web site (www.cbc.ca). First come, first served is the rule for free noon-hour concerts recorded in the **Glenn Gould Studio** (416-205-5555) for the radio program *Music Around Us*. The Glenn Gould Studio, named for the late, eccentric Toronto pianist, is also the venue for many classical and jazz concerts, as well as other special events. Reserve ahead or drop by the ticket booth, located in the lobby just inside the front door of the CBC building.

If your timing is right, you might catch a glimpse of your favorite band in the **MuchMusic** studio (CHUM-Citytv, 299 Queen West, 416-591-5757), which runs live tapings eight hours a day. There are no seats inside the studio, but you can jostle with the usual mob of young groupies who gather outside on Queen Street to gawp through the large plate-glass window, referred to by MuchMusic staff as the

"street-front environment." Cool. Citytv does offer you the chance to be part of the studio audience for *CityLine* (416-591-5757), a lifestyles talk show that airs Monday to Friday at 10 a.m. Fans of late-night talk show *Ed the Sock* can get their foot in the door by calling 1-800-3-SOCK-ME.

Rock fans will jump at the chance to squeeze into the small street-level studio at radio station **Edge 102** (228 Yonge, north of Queen, 416-408-3343) for *Live on the Edge* (recorded Monday to Friday from 6 p.m. to 8 p.m. and broadcast on 102.1 FM). Between live songs, hosts Brother and Bookie interview musicians who happen to be in Toronto for a local gig, while the studio audience swoons and cheers from the mini bleachers. Very cool.

Scathingly ironic stand-up comic Mike Bullard hosts the popular television talk show *Open Mike* (Masonic Temple, 888 Yonge, at Davenport, 416-934-4737 or 1-888-394-MIKE), which airs five evenings a week. The guest list is usually announced a week or two ahead of time, and reservations are recommended for the taping, although walk-ins are welcome if there's space. Taping takes place on weekdays from 5 p.m. to 8 p.m.

S E C R E T
SUNNYSIDE

Inspired by the success of New York's Coney Island, the Toronto Harbour Commission in the early 1920s conceived and built **Sunnyside** (Lakeshore Boulevard West and Parkside Drive, directly south of High Park on Lake Ontario), a 15-acre amusement park that was Toronto's favorite attraction for more than 30 years. There was no admission fee, and the city even paid for free streetcar rides across town so that children could swim at the beach. In 1924, folks crowded the park to watch bathing beauties compete in the very first Miss Toronto contest. Other amusements included baseball, Easter fashion parades along the boardwalk, Sunday-night sing-alongs, and boat-burnings, when old wooden ships were set ablaze offshore. Today, the old merry-go-round and giant roller coaster no longer exist — the park was pushed out of the way in the mid-1950s by Canada's first urban expressway, now known as the Gardiner (possibly slated for demolition itself, in the not-too-distant future) — but a few landmarks remain. The grand **Sunnyside Bathing Pavilion** (1755 Lakeshore Boulevard West) originally contained two dining rooms and two tea gardens that opened into a dance floor, while the change rooms below could accommodate hundreds of bathers. The building has been partially restored in recent years, and the **Sunnyside Pavilion Café** (416-531-2233) serves food and drink in the summer, but somehow it continues to resemble a deserted movie set. The nearby **Gus Ryder Sunnyside Pool** (in Budapest Park), the world's largest outdoor swimming facility when it was built in 1925, still attracts summertime bathers, and the **Palais Royale Ballroom** (1601 Lakeshore Boulevard West, 416-532-6210) still hosts big-band dances. Pedestrian access to the park is best gained via the long footbridge that arches over the expressway from the corner of King West and Roncesvalles.

SECRET
SWEETS

If Pez and gummy bears are your appetizers of choice, you'll find plenty to set you drooling at **Sugar Mountain Confectionery Co.** (320 Richmond West, 416-204-9544). The candy collection assembled here will do more than Proust's madeleine to prod your childhood memories. Sugar Mountain spreads the sweetness around, with four other outlets (571 Queen West, 1920 Queen East, 2525 Yonge, and 2299 Yonge).

The Redpath sugar company has been nurturing the Canadian sweet tooth for almost a century and a half, and the **Redpath Sugar Museum** (95 Queen's Quay East, between Yonge and Jarvis, 416-366-3561) celebrates both the history of sugar manufacturing and the Redpath family saga. Constructed on the interior to resemble a sugar crystal and decorated in gold paint, the museum displays industrial implements, domestic tableware, fancy sugar cubes, and interpretive exhibits that explore the origins of cane sugar, the refining process, labor conditions, and sugar's nutritional value. Located behind the waterfront refinery, the museum has limited hours (Monday to Friday, 10 a.m. to 3:30 p.m., closed noon to 1 p.m.), but admission is free, and tours can be arranged by appointment. Enter the Redpath complex from the Yonge Street side, and watch for museum signs at the gate.

SECRET

SYNAGOGUES

Toronto's Jewish community is largely responsible for establishing the still-vibrant Kensington Market in the early 1900s. Although the area has undergone radical shifts in population, several Jewish synagogues — at one time, there were as many as 30 — remain as landmarks. Services continue at **Anshei Minsk Synagogue** (10 St. Andrews Street, 416-595-5723), a squat Russian Romanesque structure built in 1930. Completed in 1927, the **Kiever Synagogue** (28 Denison Square) was designed by Jewish architect Benjamin Swartz with a distinctly Middle Eastern flair, featuring geometric stained glass and twin Byzantine-style domes set atop red-brick towers. Inside, the worship hall is decorated with brass ornaments and paintings that depict biblical animals and zodiac signs. An enormous hand-carved Holy Ark dominates the space. The Kiever Synagogue has been fully restored to its original condition by the Ontario Jewish Archives Foundation, and in 1979 it was the first building of Jewish significance to be designated under the Ontario Heritage Act. The synagogue stands on the former site of Belle Vue manor (demolished circa 1890), the home of affluent Torontonian George Taylor Denison.

Toronto's oldest Jewish congregation resides at **Holy Blossom Temple** (1950 Bathurst, 416-789-3291). Founded in 1856, the temple's home for the first 20 years was actually a room above a drug store on the southeast corner of Yonge and Richmond. By the mid-1890s economic circumstances had improved enough to permit construction of a proper synagogue on nearby Bond Street. It's a splendid Byzantine affair with a large central dome and domed stair towers at the

corners. In 1938, when the congregation moved north to the new Bathurst Street temple, the old one was reconsecrated as **St. George's Greek Orthodox Church** (115 Bond, 416-977-3342). Inside, where the Ark and *ner tamid* once rested, visitors will now espy a mosaic of St. George and the dragon.

S E C R E T
TEA

✤

High tea in the English tradition is served daily (2:30 p.m. to 4:30 p.m.) in the Lobby Lounge at **Le Royal Meridien King Edward Hotel** (37 King East, 416-863-9700). The fixed-price affair includes your choice of loose-leaf teas, scones with Devonshire cream, little sandwiches, and petit fours. The executive chef at the King Edward, who apparently spent a couple of years at the queen's place in London, is responsible for the Buckingham Palace shortbread. If you prefer to break a bit later in the day, the tea menu is also served from 4:30 p.m. to 6 p.m. in the hotel's Café Victoria.

In Toronto's downtown Chinatown, the **Ten Ren Tea Company** (454 Dundas West, 416-598-7872) sells a long list of imported leaves, including jasmine, oolong, long chin, semifermented green, and gunpowder tea. Herbal teas and restorative ginseng roots are also available, and the store carries a selection of the necessary implements: porcelain and clay tea sets.

SECRET

THAI

The lineups at **Green Mango** (730 Yonge, south of Bloor, 416-928-0021) move quickly, and turnover at the tables is pretty fast, so don't worry if it looks crowded. The cafeteria-style kitchen turns out surprisingly good Thai noodle combinations with fresh, peanut-sprinkled salads. A great place for a quick lunch.

SECRET

THEATER

Anyone with a passion for theater, film, opera, dance, or practically any performing art will fall in love with **Theatrebooks** (11 St. Thomas, near Bay and Bloor, 416-922-7175). Occupying two floors of a renovated brick building near the center of town, the store carries everything from histories and how-to books (such as the ever-in-demand *Acting with an Accent*, cassette tape included) to biographies, television production manuals, and illustrated guides to creating special effects.

With more than 200 resident professional theater and dance companies and upwards of 70 venues, Toronto has become the third-largest theater center in the English-speaking world, after New York and London. Each month sees an average of 75 productions playing around town, from megamusicals and children's theater to French-language and First Nations drama. Half-price tickets to many of the mainstream shows can be purchased on the day of performance at

TO Tix (208 Yonge, south of Dundas, 416-536-6468, ext. 40). The booth is open Tuesday through Saturday, noon to 7:30 p.m., and tickets must be bought in person. During the summer, a satellite kiosk is open at Nathan Phillips Square in front of Toronto City Hall (100 Queen West, at Bay).

The main TO Tix location is directly across the street from the fully restored **Elgin and Winter Garden Theatres** (189 Yonge, 416-872-5555), one of the world's last remaining double-decker theater complexes. The lower-level Elgin is a festival of gold leaf, plaster-work, and red plush, while the upstairs Winter Garden sports an atmospheric ceiling of leaves with supporting columns resembling tree trunks and trellised walls. Tours are available throughout the year on Thursday (5 p.m.) and Saturday (11 a.m.), as well as Sunday (11 a.m.) in July and August. You can also get a limited peek at the building if you attend a play or other live event, since the theaters are still in operation.

Toronto millionaire Ed Mirvish is nothing if not theatrical, although his theaters are more about showbiz than Shakespeare. His flagship department store — Honest Ed's, performing at the corner of Bloor and Bathurst — is definitely a circus. Mirvish is almost single-handedly responsible for reviving the King Street West strip of Toronto's downtown entertainment district. He began by rescuing and restoring the **Royal Alexandra Theatre** (260 King West, 416-593-0351, call 416-872-1212 for tickets), a boxy Edwardian structure built in 1906–07 by 23-year-old Cawthra Mulock, known as Toronto's youngest millionaire. Then Mirvish opened a series of adjacent restaurants, furthering his campaign to bring this area to life. The Royal Alex tends to host megamusicals like *Les Misérables*, the Canadian premieres of *Hair* and *A Chorus Line*, and more recently *Rent*, the Lower East Side version of *La Bohème*.

SECRET
TOBOGGANING

Riverdale Park (Broadview, south of Danforth) has been a down-hill favorite for well over a century, beginning with a bobsled run on the south hill that could carry skilled riders as much as half a mile toward Winchester Street. An expensive park-improvement project in the 1960s included a 50-foot toboggan slope, along with the addition of soccer fields, baseball diamonds, an outdoor swimming pool, and an ice rink. Today, tobogganers take their chances from the top of the long slope along Broadview, overlooking the Don Valley Parkway.

In Scarborough, tobogganing hills can be found at **Adams Park** (Lawson, west of Union), **Cedar Brook Park** (Markham, south of Lawrence), **Milliken Park** (McCowan and Steeles), and **Thomson Memorial Park** (Brimley, north of Lawrence). For more information on these locations, call the City of Toronto East District (416-338-3278).

SECRET
TRADING

Floor attorneys, ticker tape, composite indexes, and what it means to sell short are a few of the mysteries explained at **Stock Market Place** (Toronto Stock Exchange, 2 East Canadian Place, 416-947-4676), the information and education center of the Toronto Stock

Exchange (TSE). Installations include a global media wall, archival exhibits, and interactive multimedia kiosks. Visitors are also encouraged to exchange a bit of their own capital in the boutique, where the retail "stock" includes clothing, books, and games. The stock exchange itself occupies the third through sixth floors of the Exchange Tower, and tours are conducted every weekday. Aside from feverish trading activity, attractions include large-scale artworks by General Idea and Robert Longo.

Founded in 1852, the TSE had its first permanent home at 24 King Street East (now demolished). It moved several times before settling into its current location. Its immediate past home is now the **Design Exchange** (234 Bay, south of King, 416-216-2160), where the stock market's ornate, Art Deco façade still exists — embedded in the black glass and steel wall of the fifth Toronto-Dominion tower. Constructed in 1937, the pink granite and limestone face of the building features a 74-foot carved-stone frieze showing industrial workers. Despite the intrusive interior renovations, you can still observe many original design elements of the 6,000-square-foot trading floor, now a venue for public events and design-related conferences. Artist Charles Comfort, creator of the stone frieze, also contributed eight interior murals. The trading floor, accessible via the marble stairs just inside the front door, is open for viewing when no events are taking place. Gallery spaces upstairs and on the main floor host rotating exhibitions exemplifying Canadian achievements in architecture, fashion, graphic arts, and industrial design since 1945.

SECRET
TV
⚜

A serious collection of early-1930s microphones and a typewriter used by veteran Canadian journalist Knowlton Nash are among the many treasures on display at the **Canadian Broadcasting Corporation Museum** (250 Front West, 416-205-8605). Located just off the Barbara Frum Atrium inside the hard-to-miss blue-and-red CBC building at the corner of John and Front (directly across from the Metro Convention Centre and a stone's throw from SkyDome), the museum offers broadcasting buffs an intimate look at obsolete equipment and historic ephemera from one of Canada's now-beleaguered national institutions. Free **guided tours** of the CBC building (416-205-8605) include a look at the museum and a sashay through the costume-storage rooms, as well as a peek at the modern production facilities. If you're feeling peckish, the **Ooh La La** café (ground floor, at the back of the building) sells fresh made-to-order sandwiches and excellent espresso, which you can enjoy outdoors in summer or indoors in the atrium in front of a huge multiscreen video monitor.

The MZTV **Museum of Television** (ChumCityStore, 277 Queen West, 416-599-7339) is the brainchild of Citytv visionary Moses Znaimer (the MZ in MZTV), who has collected more than 250 vintage television sets. Worried that these "hallowed instruments" of popular culture were becoming extinct — fewer television sets from the prewar era exist than Stradivarius violins — Znaimer set about rescuing what he fondly calls "living pieces of furniture." The museum charts small-screen history from the 1920s to the arrival of solid-state electronics in the 1970s, and visitors are encouraged to contribute to the MZTV oral history project by recording their own boob-tube memories.

For those who haven't yet enjoyed their 15 minutes of fame, there's the recording booth known as **Citytv Speaker's Corner** (299 Queen West, at John). Drop in a coin and speak your mind — the most creative and controversial opinions are collated for broadcast on Citytv's *Speaker's Corner* program (channel 57).

Demystifying the process of television is a key element of the Citytv mandate. Roving camera operators and open-concept "shooting environments" are among the innovative practices City has introduced to TV viewers. Free one-hour tours of the CHUM-**Citytv** building (299 Queen West, 416-591-7400, ext. 2770) are another demystifying endeavor. The CHUM-Citytv building was originally built in 1913–15 for the Methodist Book and Publishing Company (later Ryerson Press), and the architects dressed up the exterior with a few book-related bas-reliefs and Gothic embellishments, including playfully grotesque scribes and readers. Groups of 10 or more people can take a close-up look at the building's TV operations, including MuchMusic, the news department, and other live environments. And, of course, anyone is welcome to shop at the **ChumCityStore** (277 Queen West, 416-591-7400, ext. 2523) for mugs, T-shirts, baseball caps, and just about anything else that has room for a logo.

S E C R E T
24 HOUR

The **Vesta Lunch** (474 Dupont, at Bathurst, 416-537-4318), great for fried eggs or grilled-cheese sandwiches, has the requisite late-night-diner atmosphere, even during the day. The **Forum Café** (1166 St.

Clair West, at Dufferin, 416-657-0703), at the crossroads of the Corso Italia, serves standard fare to insomniac diners.

Hidden on the outskirts of the industrial district northwest of Keele and Eglinton, **Commisso Bros. and Racco Italian Bakery** (8 Kincort, 416-651-7671) keeps the shelves stocked with all manner of imported Italian foodstuffs, while the bakery at the back turns out focaccia, panini, and fresh buns all day and all night. Cream puffs, cheesecake, stuffed cannoli, and éclairs are a few of the sweeter things available, all at very low prices. Many argue that this is also the place for Toronto's best veal sandwich. Although the folks who frequent California Sandwiches (see "Secret Italian") might hold a different opinion, at least Commisso Bros. can satisfy your craving at any time of the day or night.

Closer to the downtown core, **Mel's Montreal Delicatessen** (440 Bloor West, 416-966-8881) serves up a mean smoked meat sandwich, made with meat imported from Montreal. It's authentic, but it still ain't Schwartz's. Nevertheless, getting to the Annex to feed a midnight craving is a helluva lot quicker than driving to the Main.

SECRET

UKRAINIAN

Toronto's Ukrainian community, whose roots took hold in 1891 when settler Charles George Horetzky built his house on Bedford, has grown past the 100,000 mark, making TO the second-largest Ukrainian city in the world, after Kiev. Physical evidence of the community is visible in the many domed and ornately decorated churches dotting the cityscape. The oldest is **Saint Josaphat's Ukrainian Catholic Cathedral** (143 Franklin, north of Dupont, 416-535-9192), constructed in 1914. The church is notable for the interior paintings and for the historic altar, which was brought to Canada from Lvov.

Many Ukrainian businesses, including bakeries, butcher shops, and specialty import stores, have collected along Bloor Street, between Runnymede and Jane, to form a distinctly Eastern European shopping district known as Bloor West Village. Pierogies, cabbage rolls, and jellied pig's knuckles are never in short supply at **Durie Meat Products** (2302 Bloor West, 416-762-4956) or nearby **Astra Meat Products** (2238 Bloor West, 416-763-1093). Rye breads and Ukrainian pastries line the shelves at **Future Bakery** (2199 Bloor West, 416-769-5020), a mini-chain that first opened at 739 Queen Street West (now closed) in the mid-1940s and has busy shops in four locations, including the trendy Annex (483 Bloor West, 416-922-5875). The repertoire at Future includes delicious onion rye and a decent pesto loaf.

The permanent collection at the **Ukrainian Canadian Art Foundation** (2118-A Bloor West, 416-766-6802) embraces more than 500 works by several generations of Ukrainian artists. Admission is free (donations accepted), and the foundation is open afternoons, every day except Monday.

Typical Ukrainian crafts, such as delicately embroidered tablecloths, ceramics, and decorated pysanky (Easter eggs), are sold at **West Arka Ukrainian Book and Gift Store** (2282 Bloor West, 416-762-8751), along with folktales, children's stories, and other works. Books about cooking, crafts, and conversational Ukrainian are among the variety of titles you'll find at **Arka Ukrainian Books** (575 Queen West, between Spadina and Bathurst, 416-703-2752), located on the strip of Queen West that was an earlier hub of the Ukrainian community.

Also on the shelves, in both Ukrainian and English translation, are works by Ukrainian authors, schoolbooks, musical and religious works, and nationalist, anti-Soviet tracts. More than just a bookstore, the downtown Arka sells CDs, newspapers, dolls, and more pysanky.

The **Taras H. Shevchenko Museum** (1614 Bloor West, 416-534-8662) celebrates the life and work of the famous Ukrainian writer and collects 19th- and 20th-century decorative arts. The **Leysa Ukrainka Monument** in High Park honors another poet for her contribution to Ukrainian culture.

Folk costumes, textiles, wood carvings, religious artifacts, and other heritage objects are displayed at the **Ukrainian Museum of Canada, Ontario Branch** (620 Spadina Avenue, at Harbord, 416-923-3318). The event schedule offers lectures and workshops, often in conjunction with visiting artists. The museum is located in the **St. Vladimir Ukrainian Canadian Institute**, an active center of Ukrainian culture. Home to various opera associations, writers' groups, and women's councils, the institute contains a library, a theater, and a bookstore specializing in Ukrainian studies.

S E C R E T
UNDERGROUND

Toronto's underground downtown walkway, known as the PATH, is really a disorderly maze, a stop-and-start series of tunnels and passageways connecting a complex of bank-basement shopping malls, mostly in the financial district. The meandering PATH starts at the CN Skywalk and the Metro Toronto Convention Centre on Front

Street, passes through Union Station and the Royal York Hotel, then weaves its web northward to Queen Street, City Hall, and the Eaton Centre, finally fizzling at the Bay Street bus terminal. Oh, and there's a sideways sweep into Roy Thomson Hall, Metro Hall, and the CBC Broadcasting Centre. The trail is blazed with discreet directional signs (designed by Toronto firm Gottschalk & Ash) — the word PATH spelled out in colorful block letters, each in a different font — that are reasonably easy to spot, once you know what to look for. Granted, several major theaters and tourist attractions are easily accessible via the PATH, but mostly you'll see just shops and more shops, often repeating themselves at fixed intervals (not unlike the passing background in a low-budget cartoon). If you happen to be down under during the evening rush hour, when 100,000 workers drain out of the 50 or so office towers and make a dash for the underground parking lots and commuter links, you'll understand the true meaning of the term "rat race."

In 1978, the Toronto Transit Commission (TTC) unveiled eight works of public art in the newly opened Spadina subway line. The extension added eight new stations (from Spadina, on the east-west Bloor line, north to Wilson; a ninth station, Downsview, has since been tacked on at the upper end), and the architects collaborated closely with the artists to integrate their creations. Although the **TTC Spadina Subway Art project** was initiated to bring visual art to the "average citizen," the whole deal was almost shelved in response to an outcry against the spending of money for "unnecessary cosmetic frills." Luckily, an even greater groundswell in support of the project — along with private donations and lottery funds — prevailed, and the works were installed as planned.

While some are well placed, others are out of the way and easily overlooked. Joyce Wieland's *Barren Ground Caribou* is a prime example: the giant quilt (more than 31 feet by six feet), depicting a herd of caribou on Arctic tundra, is located at the far northern end of Spadina station (Kendal Avenue exit), where very few commuters ever go. Although it's possible to transfer at Spadina between the east-west and north-south subway lines, transferring is much more efficient one stop east at St. George. The only good reason to transfer at Spadina is to play on the moving sidewalks — the long, flat "escalators" connecting the two subway lines — or, perhaps, to view the artwork. Also at the far end of Spadina is Louis de Niverville's *__Morning Glory__*, a whimsical porcelain enamel mural intended to re-create in a dream sequence "the dawn of a new day for the early morning subway rider." If you enter via Kendal Avenue, you can see both works without paying the subway fare — de Niverville's mural graces a stairwell leading into the station, while Wieland's puffy caribou are visible through the metal bars at the bottom of the stairs.

The other artworks can be enjoyed for the price of a TTC token. Farther up the line, at Dupont, enormous plants and flowers are depicted in James Sutherland's glass tile mosaic, *__Spadina Summer under All Seasons__*. Other creations, by Claude Breeze, Michael Hayden, Rita Letendre, Gordon Rayner, and Gerald Zeldin, punctuate the northward trek, which ends at Wilson with Ted Bieler's impressive *__Canyons__*. This aluminum wall relief resembles striated rock formations that might be revealed by geological excavation.

Dead goldfish and other debris that we flush down Toronto toilets and sinks eventually end up in a sewage treatment plant, and the good folks at the **City of Toronto Works and Emergency Services** (416-392-9652) are ready and willing to show us what goes on down there, before the water is dumped back into Lake Ontario. Free tours of the **Ashbridges Bay Treatment Plant** (9 Leslie), **Humber Treatment Plant** (130 The Queensway, Etobicoke), **Highland**

Creek Treatment Plant (51 Beechgrove, Scarborough), and **North Toronto Treatment Plant** (Redway Road, East York) can be arranged by appointment only, for groups of at least five people. (See also "Secret Art Deco" for walk-in tours of the R.C. Harris Filtration Plant.) Tours must be booked at least two weeks in advance.

As Toronto expanded in the late 1800s, the landscape was ruthlessly flattened to accommodate new construction. Deep ravines were filled with earth, and the creeks that ran along ravine basins were buried in brick sewage pipes. One such underground waterway in west Toronto is Garrison Creek, named for the military post at Fort York. Eco-conscious community groups, with the aid of sympathetic municipal politicians and planners, have initiated a project to increase public awareness of Garrison Creek. Among the set of six **Discovery Walks** sponsored by Toronto Parks and Recreation (416-392-1111), the **Garrison Creek Discovery Walk** traces the southbound route of the invisible stream, starting at Christie Pits Park (Bloor West at Christie). Interpretive and directional signs have been installed to help people take self-guided tours, while four sites along the way have been spruced up with "Memory Banks" by artist John LeRoux. You can pick up a pamphlet describing each of the Discovery Walks at community centers, libraries, and information booths.

Many Torontonians have heard about the unused subway station known as **Lower Bay**, but few have ever seen it — except unknowingly, perhaps, in the movies. Opened in February 1966 beneath Bay station on the Bloor-Danforth line, Lower Bay was intended to integrate the east-west line with the north-south Yonge-University-Spadina line, allowing passengers to get downtown without changing trains. It was shut down after only seven months, due to frequent mechanical delays that interrupted the whole system. Closed to the public, Lower Bay has become a storage bin for escalator parts. It has a second life, however, as a movie set — watch for it the next time you see *Darkman* or *Johnny Mnemonic*. Another abandoned TTC project, the rough draft of an east-west underground streetcar line, languishes beneath the Queen Street subway at Yonge Street. Conceived to run from Trinity Bellwoods Park in the west to Logan Avenue in the east, the plan was shunted aside in the early 1950s when it became clear that the city's commercial center was moving north to Bloor Street. The lower Queen Street station is now little more than a segment of unfinished concrete tunnel. If you follow the walkway that goes under the tracks between the northbound and southbound platforms at Queen, you may notice a pair of unmarked red doors — if you happen to have the keys, you can sneak a peek at the forgotten past.

SECRET
UNIVERSITY OF TORONTO

The main U of T campus is spread out over a wide area, roughly bounded by Bloor Street on the north side, College to the south, Spadina Avenue to the west, and Bay to the east. From June to August, free guided walking tours depart from the **Nona Macdonald Visitors' Centre** (25 King's College Circle, 416-978-5000) on weekdays at 10:30 a.m., 1:00 p.m., and 2:30 p.m. At other times of the year, tours are offered at 11 a.m. and 2 p.m. You can take self-directed walking tours at any time, following the commentary provided by plaques affixed to many of the historic structures around campus. If you happen to be on campus during the first week of any month during the school year, don't overlook the **Soldiers' Tower** (situated at the west end of Hart House). There you'll find a second-floor display of war memorabilia, portraits, and plaques remembering the many hundreds of U of T students who served in battle, including "In Flanders Fields" author John McCrae. The Memorial Room is accessed via a doorway east of the tower.

Inside Hart House, the **Justina M. Barnicke Gallery** (7 Hart House Circle, 416-978-8398) showcases the work of young Canadians in one gallery and pieces by established artists, often drawn from the Hart House permanent collection, in the other. Another gallery worth visiting is the **University of Toronto Art Centre** (15 King's College Circle, 416-978-1838), home to the Malcove Collection. Donated by New York psychoanalyst Lillian Malcove, the gift includes a few works by Klee, Picasso, and Matisse and more than 500 mostly medieval art objects, such as Lucas Cranach's exquisite painting *Adam and Eve* (1538).

For an up-to-date list of on-campus happenings, call the **U of T events information line** (416-978-8638).

SECRET
VEGETARIAN

Chinese spring rolls, vegetable-filled dumplings, and eight types of gluten are among the choices at **Buddha's Vegetarian Foods** (666 Dundas West, west of Bathurst, 416-603-3811). All-natural herbal drinks designed to energize you and improve your mental acuity are available at **Smart Bar & Eatery** (754 Queen West, 416-504-0653), along with veggie burgers, burritos, samosas, pasta plates, and a recommended tofu cheesecake. Closed Monday and Tuesday. North of the Annex area, **Annapurna** (1085 Bathurst, just south of Dupont, 416-537-8513) serves predominantly South Indian vegetarian and macrobiotic cuisine, while Govinda's Dining Lounge in the **Hare Krishna Temple** (243 Avenue Road, at Dupont, 416-922-5415) offers inexpensive lacto-vegetarian cooking amid swirls of burning incense.

Kosher vegetarians might like the crepes, blintzes, and vegetable cutlets at **Milk 'n Honey** (3457 Bathurst, near Lawrence, 416-789-7651), while vegetarians who like to imagine otherwise will find lots of mock-meat dishes at **Bo De Duyen** (254 Spadina Avenue, south of Dundas, 416-703-1247) in Chinatown.

Noah's Natural Foods (322 Bloor West, at Spadina, 416-968-7930) is primarily a retail store, but there's a cozy three-stool café inside with take-out vegetarian fare. **Vegetable Kingdom Organics** (443 Adelaide West, 416-703-6447), as the name suggests, carries organic fruits and vegetables, as well as whole grains, beans, and other groceries. **Baldwin Natural Foods** (20 1/2 Baldwin, in Kensington Market, 416-979-1777) sells organic fruits and vegetables, vitamins and mineral supplements, and bulk foods. The **Big Carrot Natural Food Market** (348 Danforth, near the Chester subway, 416-466-2129) is probably the largest outlet in TO, but it may also be the priciest. There's a take-out snack bar inside selling such delights as quinoa salad with fresh cilantro.

The **Toronto Vegetarian Association** (2300 Yonge, 416-544-9800, www.veg.on.ca) organizes an annual **Vegetarian Food Fair** at Harbourfront's York Quay Centre (235 Queen's Quay West, 416-973-3000), usually in early September. There are cooking demonstrations and free food samples, a vegetarian and organic food marketplace, health and nutrition information booths, musical entertainment, and activities for kids. Admission is free.

SECRET

VIDEOS

If a spanking big Blockbuster video store hasn't opened in your immediate neighborhood yet, wait five minutes. But if you're tired of watching Hollywood schlock and expurgated versions of independent releases, you might find something more engaging at one of Toronto's alternative video outlets. Foreign and Canadian film classics and uncut independents are available at **Revue Video** (207 Danforth, at Chester, 416-778-5776). They even stock documentaries — for a change of pace, check the metaphysics section, the art shelf, or perhaps the gay and lesbian studies collection — but don't expect to find any A&E Biographies.

Film noir and anime aficionados flock to **Suspect Video** (619 Queen West, 416-504-7135), while sister store **Suspect Video and Culture** (605 Markham, 416-588-6674) supplies film 'zines, posters, and books in addition to video rentals. Just inside the door, the display case sets the tone with plastic dragons, a pair of GI Joes in a friendly embrace, and similarly crucial evidence of pop culture. Suspect rents out true classics, including the complete Andy Warhol opus, Hong Kong action epics featuring Chow Yun-Fat and Jet Li, a delightful assortment of old-school kung fu flicks, B-movies galore — and every other category from C downward. Simply browsing through the racks of forgotten horror films with wildly creative cover art is far more entertaining than actually watching most mainstream Hollywood products.

SECRET
VIEWS

Okay, so you know about the CN Tower. Where else can you get a good view of the city? **Panorama** (55 Bloor West, 416-967-0000), on the 51st floor of the Manulife Centre, boasts the city's highest licensed patio, permitting you to actually step outside with a drink in your hand (depending on your affection for heights, that may or may not be a good thing). Inside, the decor is apparently intended to remind you of South America, with its Brazilian cherrywood tables, Latin murals, and exotic artifacts, but the look achieves more of an airport-lounge effect. Never mind — order a Scotch and savor the 360-degree view.

You can enjoy classier digs, good food, and a slightly higher vantage point at **Canoe Restaurant + Bar** (54th floor, Toronto-Dominion Bank Tower, 66 Wellington West, 416-364-0054), an upscale downtown spot favored by bankers and traders. Floor-to-ceiling plate glass on the south wall provides a commanding view of Toronto harbor, only barely obstructed by the Canada Trust building to the east and the thin concrete spindle of the CN Tower to the west. Bar patrons can glimpse Union Station directly below, and the swath of rail lands south of Front Street, including the semicircular John Street Roundhouse (see "Secret Beer"). Out beyond the tracks and the raised concrete corridor of the Gardiner Expressway lies the encircling arc of the Toronto Islands, separating the small ferries and sailboats plying the inner harbor from Lake Ontario's gray-silver expanse. The pricey menu at Canoe includes Yukon caribou roast, arctic char, roasted rabbit and wild mushroom soup, Digby scallops, and even a selection of sushi. It's open Monday to Friday until midnight, but

Canoe's best viewing hours are in the early afternoon, while there's still daylight and the atmosphere at the bar is casual.

A mere 18 floors up, the **Rooftop Lounge** (Park Hyatt Hotel, 4 Avenue Road, at Bloor West, 416-924-5471) is kind of creakily old-fashioned, with '50s-style waiters, salted nuts, and walls hung with faded caricatures of Toronto celebrities like Margaret Atwood and Adrienne Clarkson. But the books, couches, and wood-burning fireplace make it a cozy retreat, and sometimes the real writers and artists even drop by. The view from the center of town looks south, and the best part is that you can step outside to enjoy it.

The **Lighthouse** (38th floor, Westin Harbour Castle, 1 Harbour Square, 416-869-1600) offers diners a revolving 360-degree view of Toronto and the lake. Open for three meals a day, including steak and seafood dinners (the kitchen closes at 10:30 p.m.) and cocktails till 11 p.m., the restaurant can be reached from the main lobby by any one of six elevators in the south tower. Take the glass-enclosed scenic elevator that rides straight to the top for a rising view north toward the city.

S E C R E T
VINYL
⚜

If you're still committed to the vinyl way of spinning discs, you can find records for sale at several downtown venues. If it's vintage rock'n'roll, doo-wop, or blues you're after, **Kop's Kollectibles/ Vortex** (229 Queen West, west of University Avenue, 416-593-8523) will provide you with a vinyl fix from its exhaustive selection of albums and 45s. You'll also find an excellent assortment of unusual new and used CDs, ranging from electronic and world music to punk. A few doors west, you'll discover more vinyl and CDs at **Driftwood Music** (247 Queen West, 416-598-0368). You can also flip through the bins at **Penguin Music** (2 McCaul, just north of Queen West, 416-597-1687), **Black Planet** (494 Queen West, 416-504-9261), and especially **Rotate This** (620 Queen West, between Spadina and Bathurst, 416-504-8447), where the collection leans toward indie rock, acid jazz, and dance but definitely *not* classical, country, or heavy metal. Don't even ask.

S E C R E T
WALK OF FAME

What does figure-skating star Kurt Browning have in common with Walter Ostanek, the King of Polka? Both men have been awarded stars on **Canada's Walk of Fame** (416-367-9255, www.canadaswalk offame.com). Since 1998, dozens of musicians, actors, hockey players, artists, dancers, and other "national treasures" have been immortalized in our very own Hollywood Boulevard North. Stylized maple leafs, fashioned from buffed marble and granite, are embedded in concrete along a designated stretch of sidewalk in the downtown entertainment district. Officially, the City of Toronto has set aside about a dozen blocks of sidewalk, on a route that begins near Festival Hall at John and Richmond Streets, follows John Street south to King Street, crosses east in front of the Princess of Wales and Royal Alex Theaters, turns south on Simcoe Street past Roy Thomson Hall, and cuts back across Front Street to the CBC building at John Street again. All inductees to date, however, are planted along King and Simcoe Streets, so if you want to go stepping from star to star, you won't need to walk more than a long block or two. On the upside, all that unused space means you still have time to get famous and maybe earn your own star in Toronto's cement heaven. There's an annual gala honoring new inductees, and when the celebs come out for the official unveilings, there's always an adoring crowd.

S E C R E T

WAREHOUSES

Most of the large warehouse buildings south of Queen Street West near Spadina Avenue have been converted for postindustrial enterprises, primarily offices and new-media sweatshops. The typically high ceilings, large windows, and wide-open interiors also work well as studio and exhibition space, as loft-dwelling visual artists have long been aware. In this area once known as the heart of the garment trade, galleries and arts-minded organizations have gathered in significant clusters. The building at **80 Spadina Avenue** (between Adelaide and King) is home to **Gallery 306** (second floor, 416-504-7273), the **Leo Kamen Gallery** (Suite 406, 416-504-9515), and the **Ryerson Gallery** (Suite 305, 416-703-2235), among others. Near neighbors include the **Red Head Gallery** (96 Spadina Avenue, eighth floor, 416-504-5654), located just north in the Darling Building.

One block south of Queen Street West and a few steps east of Spadina Avenue, the entire building at **401 Richmond Street** vibrates with

artistic energy. Studio occupants include artists, animation and graphic design companies, hat and clothing designers, arts-related organizations (from Canadian Artists Representation Ontario to the Royal Canadian Academy of Arts), film and video festival organizers, magazines (from *FUSE* to *MIX*), theater and dance groups, and several galleries. The latter include **A-Space** (Suite 110, 416-979-9633), **Gallery 44,** the **Centre for Contemporary Photography** (Suite 120, 416-979-3941), **Gallery 401** (Suite 240, 416-506-9595), **Inter/Access** (Suite 444, 416-599-7206), **Wynick/Tuck Gallery** (ground floor, 416-504-8716), **Women's Art Resource Centre** (Suite 122, 416-977-0097), and YYZ **Artists' Outlet** (Suite 140, 416-598-4546). The stairwells, windows, and skylights are filled with hanging plants and tropical flowers, a ground-floor daycare and rooftop garden have been built for tenants, and the **Loftus Lloyd Café** (Suite 135, 416-596-7100) serves up Illy espresso, soup and fresh gourmet sandwiches, and creative desserts.

S E C R E T
WEATHER REPORTS

If you stand back far enough from the **Canada Life Assurance Building** (330 University, 416-597-1456) and look up — the intersection of University Avenue and Queen Street West is a good spot — you'll notice an illuminated beacon, a tower with a kind of box on top. Believe it or not, the electric display is more than a fanciful light show — it's a weather report. Every four hours, the latest forecast from Environment Canada is translated into the secret language of lightbulbs. Here's the code: when the beacon is green, skies are clear. Red means cloudy weather, and flashing red warns of rain. When the beacon is flashing white, the forecast is snow. Running lights on the tower signify movements of the thermometer: up means the temperature is getting warmer, down denotes cooling, and steady lights mean there's no change. During daylight hours, the forecast applies to the balance of the day. At night, it applies to the following day. Little cards revealing the weather code can be picked up in the lobby. The Canada Life building itself, erected in 1929–31, represents the Beaux Arts aspirations once harbored by city planners for University Avenue. In the early 1900s, when the City Beautiful Movement blew through North America, Torontonians envisioned a ceremonial motorway that flowed west from Union Station along Front Street and then veered north on University Avenue toward Queen's Park, the provincial parliament building seated above College Street. Sidewalks along University Avenue were widened, the median strip was beautified, and Canada Life was the first to start building. The Depression, however, deflated all hope for the grand boulevard, and the plan for a massive line of uniformly styled architecture was never realized.

SECRET

WINE

If stomping barefoot in a bucket of grapes is your idea of what it means to make your own wine, you should visit **Fermentations** (824

Pape, three blocks north of Danforth, 416-778-9000) for a quick lesson in the modern art of DIY. Since 1993, store owner Charles Fajgenbaum and his staff have been walking would-be vintners through the process and pumping out gallons of transmogrified grape juice at bargain prices. Begin by choosing juice for the type of wine you want (all grapes are prestomped). Put it into a fermenting container, and come back in eight weeks to bottle and cork it yourself. Choices include Ontario grapes from the Niagara region, as well as selections from France, Italy, Germany, and the US. At any given time, you'll have about 25 varieties to choose from, and you're welcome to customize. From an oak-fermented chardonnay to a heavy cabernet sauvignon, the choice is yours. Fermentations also does beer, with or without mash. Brewing takes about an hour, and the results are ready for bottling in two weeks. Reservations are required, however, so the staff can get the water boiling in one of the well-polished copper kettles. A beer-making session results in approximately six cases (24 regular bottles each) for about $100, while a batch of wine yields between 24 and 28 bottles (prices per batch vary from $95 to $130). If you're not a big drinker, or you don't have room to store a ship-load of bottles under the bed, you can share the wealth with your friends and family. Failing that, the store will happily find you a brew buddy.

Ordering wine in a restaurant can often set you back more than the meal itself, with markups exceeding 100 percent in some places. At **Mammina's** (6 Wellesley West, 416-967-7199), all wines are sanely priced at a mere $5 above LCBO rates. The list isn't long — about 30 Italian reds and a handful of whites — but they're carefully selected and properly stored in the temperature-controlled cellar. The cooking is plain but pleasantly executed. Recommended for lunchtime rendez-vous when you're shopping the Yonge Street strip.

SECRET

YORK

The region of Metro known as York, a key-shaped parcel of land whose western boundary follows the bank of the Humber River, has a rich past, celebrated in two historical museums. **York Museum** (2694 Eglinton West, 416-394-2759), open weekdays from 1 p.m. to 3 p.m., focuses on the city's development, while **Lambton House** (4066 Old Dundas, 416-767-5472) is a heritage building, with photographic displays and a program of lectures, workshops, and tours.

SECRET

YORK UNIVERSITY

Anyone arriving at **York University** (4700 Keele, 416-736-2100) in the late 1970s, when I was a student there, couldn't fail to notice an apparently random scattering of large metal entanglements in the open field east of the original Fine Arts building. Popular mythology claimed they were remnants of a plane crash, a roguish story reinforced by the lack of any plaque to identify them as sculptures. In reality, they were a series of works by Anthony Caro known as the *York Flats*. Three of those rusted steel sculptures were eventually acquired by the David Mirvish Gallery and are now in storage, but Caro's ***Crisscross Flats*** (1974) remains on the York campus at the north entrance to the new Fine Arts complex. Indeed, there are 30-odd outdoor artworks at York, including Alexander Calder's ***Model of***

Man (a maquette of the larger *Man*, created for Expo '67) and Enzo Cucchi's **Fontana d'Italia** (1993), a weeping fountain constructed of bronze and granite. A raised plaza between the Scott Religious Centre and the Scott Library, envisioned as a public square but rarely used by the York populace, is the site of George Rickey's peacefully kinetic **Four Squares in a Square** (1969–70): four burnished rectangles of stainless steel, mounted on a pole, that sway in the wind. Movement of another sort occurs in a nearby reflecting pool, where the five arcs of brightly painted fiberglass tubing comprising Hugh LeRoy's **Rainbow Piece** (1972) are mirrored in the water, their image shifting with the wind and sun. Other works on campus include commissions by Jocelyne Alloucherie, Rodney Graham, Brian Groombridge, and Susan Schelle. Throughout the summer, art history graduate students lead walking tours, arranged through the **Art Gallery of York University** (N145 Ross Building, 416-736-5169). A dozen of the sculptures are also described in an illustrated brochure, available (for a suggested $2 donation) from the gallery office (N201 Ross Building). Of course, the gallery itself regularly hosts free indoor art exhibits throughout the year.

York University has an excellent fine arts program, and a jaunt through the Centre for Fine Arts gives you an inside look at the creative process. Students are often at work in the upstairs painting studios or downstairs in the sculpture center. Weekly shows at the IDA **Gallery** offer fleeting glimpses of the up and coming, while an indoor window overlooking one of the **ballet studios** is a popular spot to hang out and watch the dance students going through their paces. Dance and theater performances take place at nearby **Burton Auditorium** or the **Joseph G. Green Studio Theatre**. Film screenings take place in the **Nat Taylor Cinema** and **Curtis Lecture Halls** — watch for posters plastered around campus. Student films aren't regularly shown, except during the annual end-of-year showcase, usually held during the first week in May. Films from all levels of the program are screened on campus, while graduating student films are given a second showing somewhere downtown — call the **Film Department** (416-736-5149) for details.

Like any university, York is a hive of activity, with many public events — lunchtime lectures, musical concerts, sporting matches — organized by the various colleges and faculties. You can also eat and shop in the York Lanes mall. Brief daily tours of York, including the business school, the Bethune Residence, the student center, and a few other highlights, are arranged by the **York Liaison Office** (416-736-5100). Led by student ambassadors, the tours begin at 11:15 a.m., Monday to Friday, from August to May — call one day ahead to register. Free parking vouchers are available. Tours of the Fine Arts facilities are handled by the **Fine Arts Department** (416-736-5135) and take place on Thursday afternoons.

S E C R E T
'ZINES

Canzine (416-703-4644) is Canada's biggest festival of alternative publishing culture. Comix and 'zine publishers come to hawk their wares, panels debate aspects of indie culture, indie bands perform, and readers rant from the stage in scheduled and open-mike performances. Canzine usually takes place on a Sunday in late September or early October. It's organized by *Broken Pencil* (www.brokenpencil.com), a 'zine about 'zines and the best source of information about related events.

A smaller and punkier version of the 'zine fair is **Cut 'n' Paste** (416-531-4133), launched in the early 1990s by Stacey Case — a local radio and punk-scene personality — who considers 'zines "an art form." This event, which sees about 300 'zines crammed into a downtown bar for one day every June and December, depends mainly on word-of-mouth.

'Zine buyers looking for indie publications like *Factsheet 5* and *Fish Piss* can skip the chain bookstores altogether. The best places to find local 'zines are independent outlets such as **Suspect Video and Culture** (605 Markham, 416-588-6674), **Pages Books and Magazines** (256 Queen West, 416-598-1447), and used record and bookstore **She Said Boom** (372 College, between Bathurst and Spadina, 416-944-3224, and 392 Roncesvalles, 416-532-6843).

THE SECRET FUTURE

No guidebook can even pretend to be comprehensive, especially when the objective is to unearth hidden places and previously unheard-of events. Without a doubt, some worthwhile attractions have resisted our attempts to dig them up.

In the interest of improving future editions of this book, please let us know about the sites, sounds, and tastes you've discovered that warrant inclusion. If we use your suggestion, we'll send you a free copy on publication. Please contact us at the following address:

Secret Toronto
c/o ECW PRESS

2120 Queen Street East, Suite 200
Toronto, Ontario, Canada M4E 1E2

Or e-mail us at info@secretguides.com

SUBJECT INDEX

ALPHABETICAL INDEX